PRIMARY SCRIPTURE

COSMIC RELIGION'S FIRST LESSONS

by

Sylvester L. Steffen

**FIRST BOOK
OF THE
SECOND ENLIGHTENMENT TRILOGY**

ISBN: 0-7596-3395-9 (E-book)
ISBN: 0-7596-3396-7 (Paperback)
ISBN: 0-7596-3397-5 (Hardcover)

Library of Congress Control Number: 2002111747

This book is printed on acid free paper.

Printed in the United States of America
Bloomington, IN

1stBooks – rev. 10/28/04

NATURAL LAW

The premise of "Primary Scripture" is that the essential lessons edifying all consciousness are communicated uninterruptedly in Nature, and that in their *natural* place, humans commune with divinity: the Source. Natural reason (complexity consciousness) is a self-renewing genesis. Nature's consciously enduring word/work is God's.

Introspective nature-consciousness authenticates Earthlife, but because of humankind's ignorance, arrogance, and egoistic greed and obsession, societal sensitivity toward nature has been trashed. Humankind's anti-social disconnect poisons and diseases civilizations with mortal conflicts.

The geologian Thomas Berry calls for societal awakening to an ecozoic awareness. In "The DREAM of the EARTH," Father Berry says: *"Professional education should be based on an awareness that Earth is itself the primary physician, primary revelation of the divine, primary scientist, primary technologist, primary commercial venture, primary artist, primary educator, primary agent in whichever activity we find human affairs."* (Quoted with the author's permission.)

If humankind wants to desist from its self-undoing, it needs to recapture its naturally instinctual and sustaining consciousness, relocate its societies in harmonious relationships with global Earthlife, and become a conserver of life's diversity rather than its destroyer. Next to the fundamental fact of essential, codependent relationships—the physical/moral basis of vitality and of Natural Law—all other law pales in meaning and effect.

Humans waste themselves and all Earth life unless they conform their living to the codified scripture of the NATURALIS SACRAMENTUM ORDINIS.

****

The Very Reverend John Musinsky, S.V.D., past Superior General of the Society of the Divine Word and the onetime theology professor of author Sylvester Steffen, is hopeful that a reconciliation of science and religion might help the Church be more effective in reaching people who are now more scientifically informed: *"...I would like to encourage you in your apostolate. The Church today does not know how to address modern man in such a way that she gets through to him. She will have to find new approaches. Modern man is certainly caught up in science and the approach from within his world is indeed promising."* December 5, 1999. (Quoted with permission.)

TO

FEMININITY,

THE

GROUNDSTATE

OF

ALL VITALITY.

THANKS to my wife Felicitas Angeles Garcia for her steadfast encouragement, and to all my daughters—Monica for her insight and graphic skill in capturing the soul of my labored words; Leticia for her step-by-step walking me through this work; and Veronica, Rebecca, Theresa and Maria for their ready and uplifting humor and support.

AUTHOR'S FOREWORD

In his book "Spontaneous Healing," Dr. Andrew Weil, M.D., calls for the radical reform of the medical profession (1995, Ballantine Books, A Fawcett Columbine Book, a Division of Random House, Inc., New York). By radical reform, Dr. Weil means changing the philosophical/scientific foundations of the medical profession, away from "Newtonian mechanism and Cartesian dualism." He calls for a philosophy of science that is based on "quantum physics." This writer believes that the same radical reform is needed at all levels of the educational experience, from bottom to top.

The misdirection of Newtonian mechanics and the schism of spirit and matter infect all professions with socially harmful consequences. In "Primary Scripture," a rationale for the radical reform of the philosophy of science and religion is presented.

The essential identity of soul and substance is the virtue (grace) and mark (sign) of quantum relativity. All religions must reckon in their theologies with this essential reality, whose word and work is natural sacrament with consequences in all creativity and creation. Perhaps the first lesson we need to learn from Nature's Primary Scripture is where our "self-aware bodyliness" comes from, for in our understanding of this lesson we may better understand whither we go.

Whence comes our embodied consciousness? It comes from nature. Whence comes nature? It comes from the transformational cosmos. Reason tells us that nothing comes from something that doesn't possess in itself what it produces in other. Body and consciousness are from cosmic nature. Every something (quantum) possesses the essential character of the nature and cosmos whence it comes. The transformational cosmos is itself embodied consciousness which diversifies the body-conscious unity. Each vital unity endures by virtue of the conscious complexity of embodied spirit. All body, all mass, all matter is characterized in construct (structure) and potential (energy). Every great and least quantum is a "motor" force seeking association with other motorized (spiritually driven) quanta. The trademark potential uniquely qualifying every quantum is the force that transforms it and gives to the cosmos its connectivity, continuity and relativity.

The subtlety of consciousness is qualified in quantum-electric substantiation. The micro processing of open cosmic potential gives to nature its transformational vitality. The "consciously" *intensional* forces of attraction and repulsion cause quanta to converge and diverge, and to give to creativity its potential for diversification. In the minutest first particles the will to survive is already present. The attraction of opposites, the positive-negative charge of quantum-electric particles, is the primal force of the survival instinct. Quantum-electricity is the power of construct amassed and amassing in cosmic assemblies, whose strong-force mobilizes weak-forces to serve the subtle and diverse purposes of substance-symmetry and soul-harmony. This converging and diverging dynamic, the *spiritual* power driving compositional and oppositional relationships, is essential to substantiation. The inherent positive and negative energies of quanta (substances) are with "good" and "bad" effects. Openness to essentially ambivalent discovery is characteristic of subatomic, atomic, and molecular dialogue. This electrical potential is at the same time constructive and destructive. Every quantum-electric decision is obfuscated in clouds of hidden potential, to be revealed only in the drawn-out transformations of time-qualified contingencies. Quantum-electrically driven symbiosis is a birth-process of complexity, which functionally combines the collaborative resources (material and spiritual) of substances (subjects). The recombination of disassociated substances establishes new order from chaos, while the disassociation of combined substances returns them to chaos.

Substantiation is an electrical process with positive and negative potential; it concurrently causes the molecular assembly of structures as well as their molecular disassembly. Disintegration and integration is a death and life power of spirit (soul). Substantiation is a continuity process that qualifies and quantifies; it is the death and life inter-phasing of subjectivity and objectivity.

Self-conscious subjectivity, you and I, seeks self-discovery and characterization in that which produced it (us). Self knowledge is authenticated in its identification of "that-which-is" with "that-which-produced it". This applies both to the "simplicity" of the first products of the early moments of the Big Bang and to the outcomes of the reasoned, conscious decisions of contemporary humans. Human consciousness is the subtle energy, highly qualified and far removed in its qualifications from the non-volitional intensities of the first products of the Big Bang; nevertheless, it is resourced in and from the essential continuity produced by the Big Bang. Unity-consciousness not only identifies energy in matter, soul in body, and divinity in humanity, but also, it identifies energy *with* matter, soul *with* body, and divinity *with* humanity.

At face value, it isn't evident that matter originates from and in energy, and yet Albert Einstein's discovery that matter converts to energy supports the conclusion of its origin in and from energy. Society's acculturated failure to recognize cosmic energy as the resource that makes up all the communicational (spiritual) aspects of complex matter, including its self-aware consciousness, has caused humankind to disconnect from the fact that spirit and matter are one. This has lead to the misunderstanding of the true nature of self-consciousness and to the misdirection of self-consciousness.

Consciousness (spirituality) is the essential and subtle energy of "intensionality" energizing all materiality. Together, energy and matter have coevolved over time and, in the process, have together taken on codependent manifestations that are increasingly subtle and complex.

Teilhard de Chardin uses the word "convergence," especially in the sense of the coming together of cosmic consciousness (energy-intensionality) and Christic consciousness (altruistic intentionality). His word for this is "Christogenesis." Chardin's continuity theme is with the hoped-for outcome of human consciousness rising above the mundane grind of the ephemeral to a transcending consciousness of higher purpose. As one comes to understand the *essential continuity* of cosmic evolution, the conviction becomes even stronger that altruism (intentionality) is a conscious force that is stoked by and in the natural furnace of cosmic (quantum-electric) intensionality. What determines authentic consciousness? Intention determines it. Good intention is the self-aware consciousness of quantum-electricity, *intensional inherency*, which makes decisions on the awareness of the good, namely, of that which self-preserves. Because every decision has potentially good and bad outcomes, we need to be enduringly vigilant.

Conscious intentionality is a spiritual force of self-awareness that is characterized by and in the essential continuity of outcomes. Human consciousness possesses freedom in the choices it makes. In the informed making of "the better" choices, humans exemplify inherent divinity. The Origin of allness (unqualified energy-spirituality) is the creative source that humans customarily call "God." Nature, the continuum of inter-subjective elaboration (evolution), otherwise called "creation," self-elaborates in its transformational universe. The elaboration of embodied consciousness (cosmos, creation, Earthlife) is the open work of Word (a metaphor for God). The presence of Word inheres and coheres the transformational universe. The underlying supposition of this work, and indeed of harmonic symbioses and societal harmony, is that cosmic intensionality and intentionality are the energy and the spirituality (soul) of the transformationally embodied universe. Hence, we, its issue, need to honor and live by its conscionably self-sustaining soul.

J. Wentzel van Huyssteen's "The Shaping of Rationality" (1999) presents the rationality for interdisciplinary dialogue, with special emphasis on dialogue between theology and science. In my "New Genesis Poems" (1992), "2000: A Summary Prevision toward Global Revitalization" (1998), and "Eden's Lifework Poetree" (1999), I focus on areas of cross-disciplinary urgency, areas pertaining especially to religion and science, philosophy and history. I discern in human intelligibility a natural, three-step process of rationality (communication, consciousness, conscience) by which the contrary minds of theology and science can find reconciliation.

Truth and certitude as well as intelligibility and purposeful rationality come to be realized more surely between the extremes of absolutism and relativism. The one extreme leads to the suppression of individuality (implosion) while the other leads to chaotic disconnection (explosion). Products of the first extreme include legalism, hierarchicalism and egoism. Products of the second extreme include lawlessness, anarchism and valuelessness. The conflicting voices at these extremes foment distrust and provoke the psychosomatic disease of schizophrenia.

My sense of urgency, for theology and science to seek a meeting of minds, is based in the apparent fact that the adversary voices of religion (theology) and reason (science) continue to instill a radical schizophrenia. Commonsense insists that their accommodation, and even their reconciliation, may prosper in a worldview that is experientially and evidentiarily consistent. The essential continuity of the quantum-electric universe is proposed as just such commonsensical grounding. Natural continuity can help enlighten the rationalized discontinuities of misinformation and misdirection. A reconciled worldview (transformational and acentric as opposed to the static and centrist) and the cross-disciplinary dialogue of rationality can accommodate not only the intelligence of theology and science but also that of all spiritual and intellectual consciousness. This new paradigmatic worldview well serves the commonsensical rationality of common humanity.

In March of 2000, I came across a book by a twentieth century philosopher of history, Carroll Quigley, titled, "The Evolution of Civilizations." As I read it, I began to realize that it was about the mix of historical events and their consequences to societies that I have recognized in "Eden's Lifework Poetree." Quigley's technique of historical evaluation and findings substantiate, I believe, the correctives that I'm trying to communicate.

A reading of this urgent book confirmed in me the realization of a biological conclusion and principle that needs to be impressed on public consciousness, namely, that evolutionary symbioses, in psychical and physical continuity, and advanced on the cosmic grounds of necessary relativity, tend toward civility (peaceable relationships) by reducing morphological frictions. And that the "greening of poetree vitality," by process of the trimorphic resonance of faith, hope, and love, is rationally substantiated in the soul and substance (energy and matter) processing of communication, consciousness, and conscience.

This principle and this conclusion arise from an awareness of Nature as the PRIMARY SCRIPTURE, the place and process of the revelation of the "Word," where cosmic soul/substance is validated in Word and Work, and in Natural Sacrament. Religions need to mitigate their intramural frictions, for these become amplified in the public arena and aggravate disharmony. The "process of rationality" enables the mitigation of frictions and the amplification of harmony.

TABLE OF CONTENTS

THE BIG PICTURE

In the minutest first particles, the will to survive is already in place. The attraction of opposites, the positive and negative charge of quantum-electric particles, is a primal force of the survival instinct of the elaborated consciousness of the "first parents." Quantum electricity is the energy of construct amassed and amassing in cosmic assemblies (word and work) whose strong forces mobilize weak forces to serve the subtle and diverse purposes of substance-symmetry and soul-harmony. The full potential of every quantum-electric decision is indeterminate and revealed only in the contextual transformations of time. Openness to essentially ambivalent discovery, good and bad, is characteristic of atomic and molecular dialogue occurring between atomic nuclei and electrons (subatomic particles).

Religions are about giving believable, unambiguous answers. But life's complexity does not always allow for unambiguous answers. In fact, facile answers are often counterproductive and serve rather to compound the original question by raising new questions. Perennial questions in everyone's life are: What is my origin and end? Whence come good and evil? The answers are framed in one's contextual experience. This is true for us today as it was for global peoples in diverse circumstances. Drawing universal conclusions from widely divergent global experiences has been challenging for every generation.

The various orthodoxies of belief, rooted in divergent cultural experience, often include fixed fideistic notions of privileged relationship with the creator (gods). Christianity is no exception. What seems unusual, indeed arrogant, is Christianity's discrediting of the authenticity of divine association in the experience of indigenous peoples. Challenge to Christian fideist fixations comes in recent times from general public movement toward a scientifically informed conclusion of the evolutionary diversification of life on Earth. Christian faith today is an evolved product of an ancient Judaic-Christian scripture and tradition, which convey a seven-day account of the direct creation of the cosmos and all life occupying it. The literal understanding of this account, expected of the faithful by many Christian denominations, is flat-out irreconcilable with the evidence and conclusions of the essentially connected cosmos to all life. The debacle over evolutionary continuity remains the defining issue between science and religion.

In the main, literal interpretations (fundamentalist and foundationalist) of Genesis argue that the evidence for an evolutionary continuum is too riddled with gaps to be believable. For the priest/scientist Pierre Teilhard de Chardin, out-of-step with Catholic tradition, the links of evolutionary continuity are more conclusive than the alternative of the direct, independent acts of a creating God.

Chardin was frustrated and chagrined by the blind intransigence of official Church to the evidence of evolution. While there are temporal, biological gaps in the evolutionary evidence, it now seems that even these are bridgeable in the gene mapping of present-day flora and fauna. Genes are expressed in DNA coding. The several chemical constituents of DNA are the same for all life. (Diversified life is characterized in the sequencing of the bases, C, T, G, and A on the DNA helix. Each and every cell of every living creature carries within it its specific DNA code, parentally received.)

In its root sense, evolution means *genesis*: the ongoing interdependent processes of birth, growth, decline and death, generation after generation, as allowed by the natural openness of life's gene-coding *texts*, ever accommodating to the *contexts* of time and place. Teilhard de Chardin's term "cosmogenesis" includes the ever-changing contexts of energy, matter, and place across astronomic and geologic times. His term "anthropogenesis" includes the evolutionary ascendance of sentient life to the ultimate conscious achievement of human self-awareness. His "Christogenesis" includes humankind's evolution of a God-consciousness in the continued rebirth of God-conceptioning based on updated understandings of natural relationships discovered in nature, where God's revelation is discerned. Individually, we each acquire "God's Word," in text (genetically via nature) and in context (memetically via nurture), in subjectively unique ways. Individual consciousness, though subjectively unique, is functionally common in process because of the evolutionary continuity of genetic and memetic rationality.

The concept of God is a developed consciousness about the original *being, power, or force* responsible for bringing into existence all being and becoming (creation). Communal, commonsense consciousness of "God" is still a consciousness-in-process, which is an ever transformed and transforming product and process of consciousness-ascent. God's revelation is in conscious experience. Full-bloom religious consciousness, e.g., God-conceptioning, is a commonsense processing of collective, communal rationality, subjectively informed. And, just as personal rationality (in *text* and *context*) accounts for individual God-conception, so communal rationality accounts for a *transcendent* (handed-down) God-consciousness. Static, fixated understandings, whether, of the cosmos, of human consciousness, or of God, are partial understandings that arise because of gradual learning and change. Fixations in mind give rise to conflicted human understandings rationalized in a given context. Contexts change. Fixations in consciousness are like frictions in tectonic plates. Rough fractures along fault lines prevent their natural shifting. When tensions build to the breaking point, the plates break free and shift. The rough jolting caused by tensions overcoming the friction causes earthquakes.

Static religion is loaded with tensions of frustrated consciousness. Religious consciousness is being shaken. The breaking point has been reached and the old staticisms are breaking up. The absolutist consciousness of God that has been adequate to understandings in the past is no longer adequate. Contemporary God-consciousness is the Word-expression of nature's open diversification (process-evolution). In ever-changing ways, nature expresses God-presence. Human purpose means to be God's purpose. Human word and work means to be divine Word and Work. The continuity of Word and Work is optimized and maximized in informed intentionality, individual and communal.

This awareness is at the heart of Christian awareness; namely, that Godlikeness is interpersonal Love. Consciousness of what is *ideal* (God-likeness) bears directly upon the substantiation of the *real* (human and secular). Misdirection in the real world evidences a falling short from the ideal. Facilitating greater harmony between the ideal and the real is the *purpose* of word and work, and of sacrament. As *intentional* participants in word and work, we engage God's presence within us and function as the advance agents of life that follows, recognizing in newborns the coming-again of divinity, of conscious ascendancy in newness.

Antithetical Religion

The religious vogue of staticism, centrism and absolutism is contrary to the thesis of primary scripture—life's evolutionary history. The scripture of cosmic consciousness reveals a universal continuum that is transformational, acentric and relative in energy and matter. The false presumptions behind the contrary *isms* are antithetical to authentic relationships and religion. In energy and substance, *transformational Earthlife* tends toward greater subtlety (complexity, diversity and interdependency); *acentrism* enables equivalency, redundancy and diversification; and, *relativity* comes to be subjectively expressed ever-more essentially in the diversified co-dependencies of soul and substance. Because *staticism* falsifies communication, it is antithetical to faith; because *centrism* falsifies consciousness, it is antithetical to hope; and because *absolutism* falsifies conscience it is antithetical to love. The practice of antithetical religion quashes trust and frustrates civility; pessimism and desperation root in it.

The motivation behind Pope John XXIII's convocation of the Second Vatican Council seems to be from his acute awareness of the need to lift Church and society from the global overcast of despotic pessimism and desperation prevailing in the nineteenth and twentieth centuries. Monarchical arrogance prevailed in Europe, in Church and State. Contributing to the heavy mood was the papacy of Pope Pius IX (1792-1878) and the First Vatican Council. Pius IX's papacy was the longest (1844-1878) of all times. Napoleon Bonaparte (1769-1821) was born just 23 years before the birth of Pius IX, who became pope some 20 years after Napoleon's death. In the growing and adult years of Pius IX, born Giovanni Maria Mastai-Ferretti, the Corsican Bonaparte came to be a new Caesar, dominating European politics. During the papacy of Pius IX, the Vatican lost its States, its treasured possession of a sacred, earthly kingdom. Neither the pope nor his Church accepted gracefully being stripped of their secular kingdom. (John W. O'Malley, S.J., "The Beatification of Pope Pius IX," AMERICA, A Jesuit Magazine, 8/26/00-9/2/00, Vol. 183, No. 5, Whole No. 4496, pp. 6-11, America Press, 106 W. 56th St., New York, NY 10019-3803). Out of the tenor of the times—the *super nova* era of Tridentine authoritarianism—Roman Catholicism (First Vatican Council) evolved within its leadership a reinvention of Caesarism (Czarism), along with a previously unknown "virtue," the virtue of fierce and blind loyalty to the political person of the pope. Pius IX's insistence on papal infallibility was no small contributor to this new "virtue," which also is a big trouble for our times. History shows that the institutional church accommodates to the secular order. It tends to imitate "the patterns of governance in the secular city." In the present time, the multi-national corporations "shine as tempting images for neatly ordered efficiency." This temptation is "to be watched and resisted." (Ladislas Orsey, "In Dialogue," AMERICA, A Jesuit Magazine, Vol. 183, No. 17, Whole No. 4508, November 25, 2000, pg. 15).

There seems to be some concurrence of thinking that Pius IX, although acknowledged as a holy person, was mediocre in intelligence and selectively biased in choosing people to advise him. His autocratic decision to have papal infallibility declared a doctrine of the Church is legendary. He threatened that if the First Vatican Council would not declare his infallibility, he would do so himself. In affirming his self-evaluation to the Council, Pius IX sounded very Napoleonic, "I am the church. I am tradition." On December 8, 1864, he issued his encyclical "Quanta Cura" condemning "current errors," often referred to under the catchall term of "modernism." Whatever his intellectual competence, Pius IX seems to have realized (as did Robert Bellarmine about Copernican cosmology approximately a century and a half before him) that the threats of modernity (new cosmology) were more unsettling to centrist church tradition than were the threats of all other religions combined.

Modernism was antithetical to the Church's long hallowed culture of static cosmology, centrist philosophy and absolutist theology. Pius IX believed that modernism was satanically subversive. Its evil was epitomized in the French rally cry for liberty, equality, and fraternity. Modernism was in the pope's mind the worst of times, which could only become worse under its influence. His apocalyptic vision was radicalized in Vatican I theology.

The "People Church" of Vatican II, however, has since reconciled itself with many of modernism's terms, which were anathema to Vatican I. As a result, Vatican II Church has a vision of greater optimism in the future and tends toward a theology not closed in old, backward-looking dogmata, but openly hopeful of societal change for the better. Notwithstanding Vatican II, the recidivism in our day of Pope John Paul II's papacy back to preferred Vatican I staticism, centrism and absolutism again clouds global horizons with pessimism and frustration. How dark this overcast will become and how long it will last are yet to be determined. The conflicts of the two Vatican Councils are not yet resolved.

Lesson One

First Lesson: "knowing" quantum relationship. Stated concisely, the First Lesson of Primary Scripture teaches the essential continuity of universal energy/matter—wave/particle, soul/substance—in the codependent, interrelational transformations of the cosmos. With God, as with perfected self-knowledge, "to know" is to love. God's word and work is love, as is that of life, the cosmic expression of God's love. The Call of Word is Love. Reciprocated love is true worship.

The seeding of the Universe came from a hyper-condensed, cosmic point-center, which let loose its pent-up potential in an omni-directional fireball. With this explosion a train of countless billions of new dynamic centers burst forth and continue to expand outwardly from the original center point. Even now, at any location in the universe, the expansion of new centers, grandiose and miniscule, continues simultaneously and in all directions, and point back to their point start.

Intussusception: the expanding center. The great bulk of cosmic stuff is undifferentiated "plasma" which occupies all space including the infinitesimal skies of our own body molecules. Undifferentiated cosmic plasma mothers an essentially continuous creation. Each center, each cell, is a matrix womb, the place of serendipity, of simultaneous birth/death, of resurrection/ascendance/transcendence. This reality encourages us to believe that the best is yet to come and that the future is infinitely unknowable. *("Intussusception" comes from two Latin words "intus," meaning within, and "suscipere," meaning to acquire, receive. Example: cell division is by intussusception—molecularly driven from within.)*

We are in the big picture, perhaps surprisingly to our ego-filled conscious self, of little consequence to the self-expanding purposes of cosmic stuff. We have, therefore, every reason to accept appreciatively and respectfully the little-picture role that is ours to play in the wee niches of Earth life. In its deep cosmic sense, relativity (religion) is essentially self-expressive, that is, "sexually" expressive in the essential sense of the complementarity of opposites. Artifices, under "religious" pretexts that cleave this continuous arrangement of bi-sexual self-expression, are contrary to cosmic continuity and to the nature of person, and are, therefore, misinformed in their presumptions and in their hurtful consequences. The cumulative impacts of alienation from deep nature's sexual consciousness give evidence to the social disconnect of arrogantly cultured religion and its pernicious mischief.

It is appropriate to note here the biblical usage of the word to "know," which, with reference to woman, means to have sexual intercourse with her. At all levels of communication—at the quantum-electric level, at the avian-reptilian level, at the human level—ritual and verbal exchange are used to serve the deep-knowledge purpose of social self-sustainability. Except we come to an informed sense of the "deep-sex" motivation behind all communication, we fail to arrive at a fully informed sense of our own deep psyche, which is female/male characteristic.

The organizational power of the word in its engagement of the senses—the harmonically conscious senses—is a phenomenon of higher psychical/physical complexity. Within the evolving complexity of sustainable continuity has arisen self-reflectiveness. At the quantum-electric level, the arrangement of wave/particles is an attractive/repulsive process of organization in which likes repel and unlikes attract. Patterns of rearrangement occur in electrical fields of composition and opposition. Mediating the extremes of the quantum-electric and the self-reflective are "dance-equalizers," patterns of balanced relationship that bring respondents together but also keep them apart. Many of these patterns belong to the lesser complexity of instinct. The wavefield psychology of instinct and conscious intuition are deep-grounded in the quantum-electrical. Ritual "constants" give deeper significance to verbal intercourse. Knowledge, the cumulative "science" of ritual and word, is the wisdom of deep experience.

Done in an ego-obsessive, consumerist culture, which "religiously" validates objects on the merit of money to be made on them, science itself and its cultural validation are perverted and destructively used. If science is located in the service of object-marketability, and practiced for profitability purposes, its other values fail to materialize. Consider the state of global food production and marketing. The concentration of wealth increasingly is in fewer and fewer corporations, which control the production, processing and marketing of life's necessities, always with corporate profitability as the primary objective. Such narrow control is contrary to nature, who abhors putting all her eggs in a few baskets, and prefers rather to diversify not only in the placing of her eggs but also in the varied character of the eggs themselves. This successful artifice of nature is called "biodiversity."

Because science largely serves the realm of corporate profit rather than the altruism of nature's commonweal, it functions as a power vehicle, which manipulates knowledge to a narrow and self-serving purpose. The bureaucracies of science, business, government, and even religion, are beholden to the corporate presumption of market profitability before all else. In the service of corporate profit, science becomes a prostitutional agency advocating for the exploitation of natural fecundity. Diversification is seen as an obstacle to marketing, and "science" is used to exploit diversification rather than to sustain and augment it.

Cosmic rationality. In the beginning was the communication of opposites, and with communication new "word-arrangements." Each step of communication, in substantiating cosmic transformation, was an advance of consciousness, a dance-step of "rational" purpose. Quantum-electric communication is even now the functional urgency of soul/substance. This urgency resides in the organizing polarity of quantum-electricity, and, except for the attraction of opposites and the phobia of likes for likes, rationality wouldn't be open to higher consciousness. The opposing force fields of likes disperse wave/particles in open patterns of rearrangement (like metal filings by opposing magnetic poles), and the communication of opposites in wave fields joins wave/particles in re-arranged patterns of structure and consciousness.

Wave/particle posturing is a ritual dance. Before meanings and intentions were verbalized they were expressed and stabilized in "ritualized" patterns and gestures, an accommodation given constancy by quantum-electricity. Language complexity is organized by the same cosmic intensionality as are original quantum particles. Rituals (electromagnetic dance) are gestures of intentionality perhaps more directly telling than words. "Religious" rituals, the authentication of natural gestures and experience, are "reason-driven" motions intending to enable secured passage through the labyrinths of life. Ritualizing comes naturally, for it is reason's experienced facility for negotiating life's complexity.

Informed in the basic logic of ritual, rationality edifies the whole of natural scripture. Its language speaks for all time and for all rationality no matter how complicated or how simple. Nature's wisdom-scripture composes our very selves, and except personal living resonates with nature's rationale, individuality and nature are both frustrated.

The many ways of diversification, advanced by and in the cosmic process of rationality, are the logical branches of vitality, the "tree of life," which holds all knowledge of good and evil. By intensionally "logical" structuring, diversity is sustained. "Sin" against vitality comes to the *garden* by way of the mortal consumption of sustainable diversity. If we would sustain vitality, we will come to understand and live by the established logic that sustains vital diversity, and we will avoid selfish domination that mindlessly wastes diverse species and exposes one's own to cannibalistic self-consumption.

Lessons in physics help frame the text and context of the dialogic relationship (relativity) of rationality (science) and religion (faith). The consciousness of their mutually dependent relationship evolves from communication, advanced and substantiated in quantum-electric logic. If some universal interpretation is attributable to science, it is the quantum-electric connection of process-rationality, the communicational resonance of faith, hope and love. Doing science, like doing religion, is a communication/consciousness/ conscience process. The scientist (religionist) communicates with a subject of investigation and receives information back on a subject-to-subject basis. In the exchange of knowledge the potential of change for both is realized in newly found consciousness.

The universal edifice of quantum-electric communication is an inclusionary umbrella that situates "truth" in the framework of all pursuits of consciousness (science). Quantum-electric communication/consciousness is a psychical/ physical force of continuity that puts all knowledge and structure in relationship. "Objectivity" means being factually honest about the relativity of all subjectivity. In the hierarchies of consciousness certain newly acquired insights rank by their telling of consequences which otherwise wouldn't be understood. The value of one insight over another is weighed in the consequences. The process of informing consciousness, to the purpose of making more valid judgments, is the "process of conscience." The hierarchies of value are in the hierarchies of consequences. A consciousness of high priority is the recognition of, 1.) the judgment value of all knowledge, 2.) the need to continue new acquisitions of knowledge, and 3.) the prioritizing of knowledge-values on an ethical (sustainable) framework. This is the elemental process of doing science and religion. In the venue of human consciousness, theological and scientific knowledge are intellectually proprietary (conscionable) to nature's common scripture. We "own" truth only to the extent that we are intentionally faithful in our lived expression of it.

The naturally rational process of science/religion is quantified (embodied) and spiritualized in quantum-electric dialogue, which is the work/word of rationality. Process rationality logically leads to the consciousness of cause-and-effect connections. The discovery of causal connections enables ethical judgment. Ethical judgment, while culturally characterized in "religious" consciousness, and indicative of religious conscience, is not and should not be equated with "religion." Religion is a communal commemoration, celebrated in rites and rituals, of experienced verities that enable heart, reinforce consciousness and motivate behavior that sustains essential, harmonious dependencies. Religion includes public professions and commitments of faith/belief that recite the experiential grounds of evolved (revealed) consciousness that constitute personal and communal authenticity and serve the commonweal.

In the religion/science dialogue, important questions surface, for example, does the motivation to live religiously (ethically, morally) come from knowledge or belief, from science or religion? Emotive consciousness (emotion) is a faith-consciousness enmeshed in the knowledge-complex. Reason and emotion together are motivating (informing) powers imprinted in the same neural-learning-complex. Thus, knowledge and faith should not conflict, but should, in rightly ordered consciousness, mutually serve one another. Human consciousness is the common venue in which the evolutionary experiences of life are registered and housed. The same neural tracks translate and record life's experiences, and the same electro-chemical mechanisms enmesh factual and emotional associations. Because we carry within us these wells of experience, our every new experience has a point of reference by which it can be judged. The measuring of new experience against imprinted experience evokes the intuitive reaction of affirmation or negation, depending on whether the new experience measures favorably or unfavorably against intuition.

As aspects of consciousness, certitude and confidence are experientially grounded, that is, along the course of evolutionary development, consciousness came to be informed about what was reliable, e.g., service to well-being, and what was not, and, on these understandings developed convictions of certitude and confidence, of trust and distrust.

As a quantum-electric function, consciousness is an "intensional" process of electron charge/discharge (firing) along and in the neural networks; as the products of self-aware reflection, judgment and choice are "intentional"—the word/work of intensional neural complexity. Consciousness, neurally imprinted in mind/body, tells that well-being occurs from causes, namely, from experiential relationships that reinforce individual fulfillment in communal settings. The redundancies of experience solidify the convictions of intuitional (intensional) and reflective (intentional) certitude and confidence. These are disturbed when cultural practices contradict the reliable redundancy of intuition/intention enmeshed in the evolved memory of experiences of well-being. It is a fact of experience that terrors as well as joys occur in the normal course of events, and, when certitude and confidence are shattered by persisting natural and cultural terrors, belief and trust are shaken as well.

Purposeful in helping each generation cope with the eventualities of terrors are mythologies extolling heroism in the face of adversity. Certain terrors, diseases and natural calamities, remain mysterious in their origins, and psychological coping mechanisms are helpful and necessary. In the deep past, a consciousness of higher orders of being was cultivated in the consciousness of the fearsome experiences of the unknown. Though cultured consciousness included an awareness of a higher (hierarchical) order of being(s), the dialogue of knowledge and belief ever continues the quest for certitude and confidence. Because of their practical importance, certitude and confidence continually challenge reason to secure their groundings. They can never be satisfied with intellectually blind belief (fideism) when knowledge is available to certify or debunk blind belief. Fideist impositions that claim credibility on worldviews that have lost their credibility lose their power of persuasion. Religion is credible only when its faith expectations are consistent with a worldview that is substantiated in knowledge and experience. Upon reason's credibility religion and faith depend. Philosophy, the "science" of rationality, is the discipline that informs faith, theology and religion. Philosophy is the discipline of knowledge that locates the priorities and relationships of hierarchical knowledge, old and new.

The 20th Century's cloud of philosophical pessimism fomented and fueled two fully involved world wars, and local wars almost too many to count. Such global failure of civility is something the Earth itself may not long survive. Incivility is a one-on-one relational problem that cannot be resolved globally until it is resolved individually. But, when whole nations suffer under pessimism's dark cloud, it is difficult also for individuals to be civil—let alone be infectious models of joyfulness.

Pessimism is a poison that diseases dispositions of minds. Incivility and mean-minded violence take root in poisoned dispositions of mind. The causes of poisoned minds are physical and psychological. Poisoned interpersonal relation-ships are both cause and effect of pessimism and pathologic dispositions. It isn't our intent here to go into the physical/psychological etiology of pathologic pessimism, rather, it is our attempt to focus on religion-aggravated pathologies that cloud individuals and whole societies with pessimism. Provoking religious disease are impositions of power that defraud individual/social consciousness of vital optimism that is natural to a mind at peace with itself. The cult of religion, based on fear and guilt, and administered by hierarchical power and domination, does not enable optimism and a sense of self-competency; it evokes the very opposite, pessimism and personal frustration. It is better that religion focuses on the good in the individual that can be motivated to build self-esteem and self-confidence, rather than on the limitations that are already discouraging enough without religion's put-down. The surrender of intuitional, personal faith to a distrustful contemporary power structure and the experience of institutional put-down are prescriptions for pessimism and the disabling of personal initiative.

Altruism. Communication at every level speaks of the elemental complementarity of female/male harmony. Even so, fideistic expectations are imposed on the weaker by the stronger, in family and in religious/secular culture. Experience tells that such impositions are generally not trustworthy for they are motivated in exploitation, domination and control. Family and religion (authentic, interpersonal behavior) are communal commitments of fidelity made individually by woman and man to each other. Full-hearted commitment to family/religion witnesses the communal nature of personal spirituality in its intentional choosing to live communally life's process of personal affirmation. Religion's organized body of belief and ritual (should) celebrates and facilitates age-appropriate consciousness in its lifetime process of flowering. Every person is for a lifetime, a teacher and a learner. Both competencies need to be affirmed and informed. Informed religion should do this affirmation. Because religious belief and ritual claim to be truthful and trustworthy, their obligation to be faithful to truth—as it is informed with new knowledge—is profound and frightful. Except religion is authentically open to God's ever present inspiration in the individual person, it is likely to bruise and break consciousness in its struggle to come to full flower. The frustrating baggage of a worldview fixated in centrism and hierarchicalism is a dead weight to spirituality informed in distributive, subjective consciousness.

Fideistic centrism frustrates faith and reason. A society that suffers from object-fixation is one accustomed to presumptions of hierarchical "objectivity" and not of egalitarian subjectivity. Altruism is motivation that looks beyond self-interest and to the interest of the common good. Except individuals experience good personally, they are not enabled to administer good to others. Though much good is vitiated by selfishness, it is nevertheless true that sufficient good is accessible to provide for the common necessities, if there is a personal will for distributive fairness. Service in the common good is a one-on-one endeavor. General well-being doesn't happen unless individual well-being happens. In the experience of well-being, spiritual as well as material needs must be met. When individuality is reinforced, individuals will discover in themselves personal resources for doing good. Such interpersonal commitment is the sacrament-mind of symbiosis, which does good not merely at the instinctive (unreflective) level, that is *ex opere operato*, but at the intuitional (reflective) level, *ex opere operantis*.

To experience ascendancy's uplift to a "new phylum of love" we must uplift our own and others' awareness of service to a level of personal commitment and live by the motive of love—as the religious visionaries of many cultures call us to do through history. Such commitment calls us to learn altruistic living and to teach others altruistic living. This is quintessentially the Christian Mandate.

Lesson Two

Second Lesson: the lesson of valuated relationship evolves experientially and logically from the First Lesson. Self-conscious experience motivates the

self to do those things which further and sustain the self's well-being. *Briefly stated, the Second Lesson of reflectively conscious creation is altruism, personal and social self-motivation rationally intending and actually doing the well-being of self and other.*

Well-being is a continuing process, not a static condition. If the fixations of rationalized staticism (semper eodem) and absolutism (Roma locuta, causa finita) are presumptions now stripped of credibility, then, their opposites, dynamic change (transformation) and subjectivity (relativity) are more credible alternatives. Because every individual has the power to cause changes, good and bad, the individual can no longer bask passively in the security of "religious" fideism by which one is fixated in institutional centrism/absolutism, comfortable as it may be. Daily circumstances demand individual choices/actions, which, in the specific, are mostly not enlightened by church's staticism/absolutism.

Conscious choice (morality) is in practiced choosing qualified by the consciousness of individual relationships, which is to say, a consciousness of the consequences of the choices made and of the actions taken. The consciousness of relationship that the religion/science dialogue can bring to humankind is a consciousness of rationality (intelligibility) that opens the individual and society to an ever-hopeful future, which is sustained by and in transformations mutually and collaboratively experienced with others (love).

Informed in the openness of quantum-electric truth, humankind can awaken to a sea change in consciousness, namely, from fideism to faith, from credulity to reason, from absolutism to relativity, from fixation to transformation, and, from obsessiveness to altruism.

Culturally imprinted staticisms and absolutisms are the stock-in-trade of mercantile religion, object-obsessed in kingdom building (the small-world, *Petrine* mentality). The "Petrine Church," yet flawed by Peter's worldly ambition for kingdom building, is a *lucifer* fast losing its light. But what surfaces now stronger than ever is the solid sense of the "Johannine Church," enlightened by the insights of John, the beloved of Jesus, as the authentic form of open and sustainable unselfishness. When the People Church (Johannine) motivates itself in an awareness of the personal equality of grace-possessed individuals, it will gradually mitigate the damage done by the mercantile church and bring to an end the harsh domination of patriarchism. Such an outcome is rational and moral for it prefers otherness to selfishness and distributive centering (subjectivity) to possessive centrism (objectivity).

It is instructive to set side-by-side the opposite characteristics of the static/centrist "Petrine Church" (Vatican I) and the transformational "Johannine Church" (Vatican II)

Vatican I Church	Vatican II Church
closed authority	distributive authority
fideistic	faithful
literalist	relationally open
objectivist	subjective
static	transformational
God/me emphasis	God/Other/me emphasis
legalistic	trustful

When inauthenticity prevails, its poison infects in unsuspecting ways. One poison is the estrangement of people on damaging and inauthentic presumptions about female/male sexuality. This estrangement is especially pernicious, for, children are its direct target. In turn, they pass on the poison and its consequences to their children from generation to generation. By association children acquire the diseased dispositions of parents and the prevailing culture. The manifold inauthenticities of patriarchism are so habituated in culture as to go largely unrecognized for their profound damage. A recent shock to American culture has been the increasing incidence of mortal violence perpetrated by children on each other and on authority figures, including their parents. What failure of upbringing is causing this? Isn't it caused by failures of family/social culture? In what ways are men and women failing each other and their children? In what ways are societal institutions, churches, failing men and women? Families?

A recent article by Christine Hoff Sommers, "The War Against Boys," ATLANTIC MONTHLY, May 2000, is provocative. Sommers examines the 180 degree turn around by the Harvard academician (first professor of gender studies) Carol Gilligan, who, in 1982 advanced her conclusion that school age girls are being disenfranchised because of preferential treatment given to boys. In 1995 professor Gilligan moved to the opposite conclusion that it is the boys who are being educationally disenfranchised. It is Sommers' finding that Gilligan had no evidence to support her popularized first conclusion, and for that reason, she should not now be trusted in her most recent conclusion.

For a period of more than ten years Gilligan's first conclusion was widely accepted by feminists committed to the proposition "that our society is unsympathetic to women" (pg 65), whose lobbying resulted in changes of distributions of public funds. In either event, Gilligan probably isn't completely wrong when she fingers engrained patriarchism as a contributor to the educational disadvantaging of boys as well as girls. According to the article, Gilligan advocates for women to take more control over child upbringing because of patriarchal inauthenticity. Sommers, on the other hand, finds that the problem more likely stems from the failure of paternal involvement in the upbringing of children—too many single-mom families and too much neglect of parenting by dads. Parental bonding and commitment to family are seemingly in decline. Why? Is the cult of inauthentic religion a factor? Is it a major factor? Societally, men and women together grow up suffering from too little personal/social experience of altruism in their own upbringing. The cultural emphasis on competition more than on cooperation perpetuates a social focus on ego-centrism, on the cult of me-first. Ego-centrism increases the toxicity of consumerist passion.

Altruism, the culture of concern for others, is the highest form of authentic self-interest, for, when personal interest focuses equally strong on the interest of others, one comes to be secured in the net of relationships of likeminded individuals. But when personal interest is unhealthily too self-assertive, one becomes estranged from the secured support of others. To live estranged is to die estranged. To live affirmed by others is to die affirmed by others. The perpetuated relationship of affirmation is heaven; the perpetuated relationship of strangement is hell.

The Christian is reminded that in the dispensation of love—in which all are born and called—all law is fulfilled. An encyclopedic complex of legalistic prescriptions that imprison the spirit isn't needed to control personal living; rather, we are called to live open to the spirit and to embrace God and all other in the service of love. Therein is fulfilled the scripture and the law. Legalism is soulless. Consciousness shouldn't suffer the violence of being the battleground of two churches competing for our allegiance. The way of light, of love, is the way of openness and freedom; the way of darkness is the way of slavery to legalistic fixations, of estrangement. The way of light is the way of affirmation—heaven; the way of darkness is the way of denial, of estrangement—hell.

NATURE'S PARADIGMATIC FORMAT

The "trimorphic" artifice of presenting material here under the headings of communication, consciousness and conscience is for the rational purpose of edifying ever, new faith, hope and love. Such personal edification is to a Godly purpose, i.e., to engage the paradigmatic lessons of Primary Scripture in personal, conscionable living. God's intention, as naturally discovered in the "original Word," is to self-fulfilled living. In life's processing of God's Word, the advance of harmonious transformation proceeds sustainably, i.e., by way of a naturally evolved mechanism—symbiosis. Symbiosis is the functional harmony of collaborative effort, that is, of the resonant-consonant-consilient accommodation of vital agencies with each other. Civility, the mechanism of collaborative society, roots in symbiotic living, in the resonance of trimorphic harmony.

The edification of human community is the word/work of paradigmatic nature, which is the joined process of trinitarian spirituality and trimorphic materiality. The unity of cosmic spirituality/materiality is expressed in "trimorphic resonance." No matter the complexities involved in the transformational continuum, they all originate in the 3-step "debris" dance of subatomic resonance and continue by the 3-step consilience of atomic/molecular harmonics. Even the most advanced subtlety is a complexity, which preserves essentially the foundational texts of Primary Scripture's original writing.

Paradigmatic nature is the transformational model of changing complexity. Life's structure is accounted for in the trimorphic resonance of subatomic, atomic and molecular synergisms. Resonance substantively inheres energy's intensional dynamic of molecular cohesion (mass) and coheres intentional consciousness (soul).

Neither civility nor civilization advances except by the energetic processes of communication, consciousness and conscience—the process of reason, of rationality. The motivating energy of authentic civility/civilization is the natural spirituality (quantum-electric relativity) of self-aware/other-aware consciousness. The unity of civility/civilization is the unity of word/work, of natural sacrament, the individuality/communality of essential "cosmic" continuity.

These "new genesis" writings are for the future-thinking purpose of achieving greater symbiotic civility, by which individual and communal life realize together their greater potentials. Upon the logic of this intent, i.e., the affirmation of universal well-being, the syllogism arguing for trimorphic resonance is premised. It goes: Heart and soul, we quest the greater good; but, quest is achieved only by action; therefore, heart-and-soul action achieves the greater good.

Absent work, word is empty of consequence. The essential relatedness, the reciprocal relationship of word/work, characterizes universal "sacrament," the word/work of sacred remembrance. Heart-kept in every cell of the body is the genetic code of life's common ladder, DNA—the "word-continuity" in all vitality. Word-continuity is the subsidiary grounding of the continuous process of word/working, of civility ever in process of reconciliation.

Word/working begins in family, in the committed relationship of male/female, in intent and action. Families become communities; communities become societies—civilizations. "Dance" is the best metaphor and the best action expressing intentional harmony. It begins in the harmonic relationships of man and woman, of man-woman-child. In word/work, dance expresses and accomplishes communally the trimorphic resonance of family. In trimorphic harmony, communities manifest the presence of trinity godhead. In the conscionable consilience of personal relationships, service to the greater good—universal priesthood—is exercised. The common origin of every person in quantum-electric relationship, in water, gives to every person's life common purpose, and signs in every person the same priesthood. This is paradigmatic nature's scripted word. It is inerrant. It resonates in Jesus' mandate: "Go teach all nations in the Name of Faith, Hope and Love—in the name of Father-Mother-Child." This mandate is the way to personal renewal; and, the reading of the Word in the light of updated, cumulative insights into Creation is an ever-renewing resource in the Third Christian Millennium. Heart and soul, let the dance begin!

Communication

The work of faith. In this writing, "Primary Scripture: Cosmic Religion's First Lessons," are laid out essential bases upon which a reconciled understanding of the continuity-fabric of human consciousness—the unity-fabric of religious (faith) and intellectual (reason) truths—may be grounded and secured against the inauthentic schisms of ego-capitalized rationalization.

Communications of new truths, advanced and discovered in self-aware processes, are edifications found in natural scripture. Nature's rational processes (psychical/physical) possess the inherent power and the coherent grace that can uplift self-aware Earthlife (humankind) from its stalled and backward-looking worldview to a forward-looking and transformationally energized worldview. The truly "religious" insight resonates with nature-driven consciousness.

The case for such changed consciousness was made by Vatican II in "Gaudium et Spes": *"The human race has passed from a rather static concept of reality to a more dynamic, evolutionary one. In consequence, there has arisen a new series of problems, a series as important as can be, calling for new efforts of analysis and synthesis."* Introductory statement, No 5, para 4. (emphasis added).

Consciousness

The work of hope. In "2000: A Summary Prevision Toward Global Revitalization" this author "confesses" to the bishop of his Archdiocesan Cathedral Church and to the Primate of Rome his personal faith propositions, and he identifies that from which personal and communal conversion is needed and to which all humanity must be converted, namely, from distrustfulness and self-preference to trustworthiness and equal concern for one another. In his public confession he seeks to liberate the instinctive authenticity of all subjectivity, including the collective consciousness of world religions seeking common expression in common witness.

A raised consciousness of the widespread distrust that prevails and of the destructions caused by it, but also, antidotes for distrust are presented in the "2000: A Summary Prevision toward Global Revitalization."

Conscience

The work of love. In "Eden's Lifework Poetree" this author reveals a coherent and globally vitalizing vision of soul/substance-unity and a transformational consciousness of cosmic creation's "essential continuity."

Conscionable love is the resonant chord that produces good consequences and that makes unitary sense from new communications and raised consciousness. The holistic story unfolding in nature is creatively and factually detailed in the cosmologic, philosophic and theologic trilogies of "Eden's Lifework Poetree." No one denomination or ideology can lay proprietary claim to common graces bestowed upon cosmic/human rationality. In the commitment to consilience, all religions can become bearers of grace to one another.

Let the serious dance of religion and science begin on the continuity grounds of cosmic harmony. In the contextual joining of the process of theology—discernment of the Word in Creation—with Albert Einstein's *General* and *Special Theories of Relativity*, this author seeks to illuminate a new consciousness upon which the renewal of global societies can be realized. From the equivalency of energy/matter, stated in Einstein's famous "cosmic" equation, the unity logic of soul/substance is advanced—a consistent rationale underlying resurrection, ascendance and transcendence. Generational life's experience of *resurrection* (communication) grounds religious faith; of *ascendance* (consciousness) grounds hope; and, of *transcendence* (conscience) grounds love.

"In the end," as Scripture says, "love alone endures." Communication, consciousness and conscience are the generators of Cosmic-Work-Continuity—the family tree inheritance of the Word-Made-Flesh—and the intentional revelation of the Trinity Godhead. While death dissolves all individual life, dissolution is but a phase of vitality's seamless weaving that enables life ever and again to arise freshly renewed—transformed.

In reading Pierre Teilhard de Chardin's *noogenesis* onto Einstein's quantum-electric cosmos, humankind is seen as an essential, natural transformation of cosmic continuity; to use Chardin's words, subtle Earthlife's continuing genesis is the ongoing processing of "cosmogenesis/anthropogenesis/Christogenesis." "Noogenesis" (mind-birthing) is Earthlife-consciousness ascending in life's ever resurrecting Word/work; in process of becoming ever more diversified and complex, *mind-birthing* is now a consciously networked agency of Earth sacrament whose greater perfection is enfleshed in the Sacrament (holy purpose) of Jesus Christ—the empowerment of Trinity expressed in human personhood.

"Eden's Lifework Poetree" develops Chardin's *cosmogenesis* in a NOVO-GENESIS Trilogy, his *anthropogenesis* in a METAGENESIS Trilogy, and his *Christogenesis* in a THEOGENESIS Trilogy. The "trimorphic resonance" of faith/hope/love transforms all consciousness, manifests divine relationships in communal symbioses, and is the ecstatic resonance of Trinitarian Communication/Consciousness/Conscience in human relationships.

But there is a self-promoting lucifer on the loose. The trimorphic virtues of faith/hope/love are countered by triumphal pride's antithetical vices of elitism, judgmentalism, and authoritarianism. The deceitful manipulations of *elitism* foment distrust; the harsh absolutisms of *judgmentalism* foment despair; and, the stony intolerances of *authoritarianism* foment hatreds; blind to their wasteful consequences, corporate consumerism prides these vices.

REASON FOR FAITH—COMMUNICATION

Angel Talk

Spirituality. Angel subtlety. The winged messengers filling with potential the skies of atoms and molecules are electrons. Electrons are in part composed of light sparks (photons), which are energetic components edifying physically and psychically the carbon-based structures of life. The subtleties of particulate energy, of electron (subatomic "debris") wavefields, qualify energy/matter (soul/substance) complexity. The more complex the molecule, the more subtle and complex are the potentials for greater communication and diversification.

Perhaps it is the trait of a dyed-in-the-wool optimist not to accept the cynical saw: "if you believe there is good in everybody, you haven't met everybody." The good in everybody isn't at first of its own making for it has its roots in the common genetic deep past, namely, in the phylogenic continuum of life. The "devil and the angel" in us is evidenced by the day-to-day choices that we make, which in turn are qualified by deep genetics (nature), by social coding (nurture), and by our conscious choosing (conscience).

Surely it is desirable that, as individuals and as communities, we live with integrity and authenticity, that is, in the real world consciousness of codependent necessities and of personal behavior, which enable integral and authentic living.

Faith and reason, religion and science, are integral aspects of unitary consciousness. Their harmony comes to exist in personal consciousness by the exercise of rationality, by soul/substance processing, a neural (quantum-electrical) process of mind constantly firing us within. Thinking, the process of ratiocination, is an energy-intense process of electron activity involving many brain centers, centers of memory, association, verbalization, sight, feeling, sound, taste, smell, etc. Their psychological contributions enable the integration of information processing into a reconciled, unitary consciousness. The reconciliation of consciousness takes place in the organization of information by the interactive "conversations" of nerve centers, that is, by electron activities in organized wavefields.

The ascendance of consciousness is a ladder-climb of communication advancing on the subsidiary inputs of consciousness. In the unity-consciousness of dialog, i.e., of harmonized knowledge/belief (reason/faith), the integration of science and religion is accomplished. Because institutional science and religion are sometimes worlds apart in their perceptions of truth, knowledge is conflicted in minds and many suffer irreconcilable psychological trauma as a result. Trauma arises from the conflicting voices of religion and science, which speak from the isolation of their idiosyncratic fixations. Their idiosyncratic voices agitate trauma within individuals over the assertions of "truths" which seem superficially to be irreconcilable. Except conflicts are resolved in individual consciousness, the din and dissonance of truth's conflicted voices become over time ever more shrill and deafening—"schizophrenia" is its disease.

The alienation trauma fomented by conflicted voices may originally be psychological only, but it may with time register physiologic grounding. For generations, the peoples of Western cultures have suffered aggravations of the conflicted-truth disease (schizophrenia) because of the habituated culture of animus between faith and reason, religion and science. The bridging of the schism may begin with the reconciliation of adversary religious and scientific understandings, and with reconciliation, the healing of societal schizophrenia may begin. Religion must stop its otherworld standoffishness and realize that the venue of hell, purgatory and heaven (relationship with God), is also here and now and that the way to salvation (sanitas) is by faith-shared truth, the root vitality of consciousness (hope) and conscience (love).

Natural Providence

Provident Relativity. Transformational relationship. In the quantum-electric universe there is a relationship of unity composed of and composing energy/matter/time/space. These are the four obvious dimensions of cosmic continuity. In the universe the concept of "place" is characterized in the relationships of these dimensions, as is consciousness. Place and consciousness are experiential relationships defined by the time/space of a human lifetime. This conscious relationship is "transcendent," is teachable, that is, its imprint of purpose inheres in self-awareness and transmissibly coheres matter's disposition in space/time. Teaching/learning is the transmission process.

The purposeful, transformational dynamic of energy/matter/space/time is a "religiously" energetic relationship celebrated in the rituals of "sacrament"; their relationships are embodied in the scientific word "relativity," which states the unity origins and psychological/physical identity in the quantum-electric dynamic of energy/matter.

In a series of public addresses (General Audience, Summer 1999), Pope John Paul II has introduced the concept of relativity (relationship) into the traditional religious subject matters of hell, purgatory and heaven. What is unsettling to the static notion of their "place," as traditionally described destinies for the human soul after death, is that His Holiness made clear his understanding that they (e.g., heaven) are not "places in the clouds," but are descriptions of relationships with God. All transformational relationships, including all human relationships, work because of relativity. In the specific, relativity, relationship in the specific, is an essential aspect of Providential necessity that essentially substantiates but is yet subsidiary to and consequent from prior transformations; prior relativity is the qualifying agency of successive relativity, of relationships-in-process.

"God" is perhaps best understood in nature's gratuitous agency of providence. Prior relativity is subsidiary to (antecedes) successive relativity, and the temporal process of transformational relationship is in the time/space, composition/disposition of essential continuity. Thus, the unity and continuity of transformation is the "place," i.e., the time/space of relativity in the given moment—whose consciousness of Providence is in the consciousness of relationships, the relationships that embody in a lifetime, hell, purgatory, heaven, and the enduring consciousness of Love—God. The processing agency of resurrection/ascendancy/transcendency is Word, the Logos of communication (faith), consciousness (hope), and conscience (love).

The Unacceptable Prophet

Ignorance & arrogance: genetic proclivities. Pride-bound, each of us is a walled city. Ignorance and arrogance are willfully cultured walls of separation that have genetic roots. The prophets pound on these, generation after generation. Proverbially we are told, however, and in our own experience we know it, that prophets are not accepted in their own place and time. Because the instincts of self-affirmation include motives of self-promotion it is perhaps prudent to adopt a cautionary attitude toward anyone who confronts traditionally hallowed beliefs and practices. In general, one must conclude that skepticism toward the counter-cultural preachments of anyone is healthy because too many would-be prophets are opportunistic "lucifers" promoting their self-advantaging schemes. Thus, it is probably just as well that free advice is mostly not much valued and even less followed.

The authenticity of the true prophet comes to be determined only by the test of time. In downplaying the assaults made against it, culture exposes its measure of its own authenticity and inauthenticity. It is by culture's engagement in dialogue with the countercultural that truth comes to surface. If the truth that surfaces reaffirms prevailing culture, then, the rejection of the prophet is justified; but if truth is on the side of the prophet, and the prophet is rejected, the culture will, because of its ignorance and arrogance, play out its own self-disintegration.

A 20th Century prophet who is not yet given his full due is the theologian/scientist Pierre Teilhard de Chardin, S.J. Chardin remains unacceptable even to many in his own Jesuit Society and to his Church, even though Church sanctions against him have been removed. Posthumously, I've come to know him and I choose to advocate for his prophetic message. For what it is worth, I vouch for the truths I find in his urgent writings. In the least, Church and modern culture need to dialogue openly with his counter-cultural insights. While I claim no professionalism, I do claim the conscionable right and obligation to live and represent truth as it comes through to me. May my representations about Chardin serve him well.

"Stir, Boil and Brew!" (Mythological Romanism)

In the evolutionary memory of mythological consciousness, the experience of contentiousness is portrayed in handed-down stories sometimes put in settings of wizened women in a circle around a boiling pot containing most uncommon mixtures. As they mix and boil their brew they chant nasty spells, which become the empowering spirits of the caldron contents. These spirits go about instigating mean trials on unsuspecting children as they grow up. The turns of the stories are varied to allow for different lessons. But themes recur allowing for variety and embellishments; for example, the malice of humans in societal rivalries—and the ultimate good that comes from the forces of nature, and vice versa. In the "Wizard of Oz" story one may find evil civilizational forces warring with good natural forces. The "North/South" Fairy Godmothers might be interpreted as personifications of Earth's North/South polar forces, while the "East/West" Evil Witches might be understood as personifications of conflicting currents between and amongst civilizations.

Myths, though developed in the experience of traditions and the insights of the writer, like good poetry allow for open interpretations depending on the individual consciousness of the reader. Other stories may be variations on the theme of the blame-game, the most notable of which, for example, is the story behind the original sin of the first parents in the Book of Genesis. Adam points the finger of blame at Eve, and Eve points the finger of blame at the serpent—the giant worm of consumptive appetites—which in enticing words deceptively foretells humankind's collective fate in coming to knowledge of good and evil.

It is vital that the mixing pot of ideas does not stagnate. Personal and social frustrations are the product of stagnation. A child is not born frustrated, (s)he grows up frustrated, which means to say that the frustrations that arise from cultural fixations may, for example, lead to self-destructive actions for the lack of imagination that inspires a sense of fulfillment in serving the commonweal. As we should now be well aware, a frustrated child may become a time bomb that eventually goes off, tragically destroying him/herself and others. A version of the Cain/Abel story all over again.

Is mythologized Romanism failing? Two questions before answering that: What is "Romanism," and what is meant by "failing"? Romanism includes that which fundamentally characterizes classical Greco-Roman culture and institutions. In the unequivocal opinion of the philosopher of history Carroll Quigley, in "The Evolution of Civilizations," that which gave rise to classical Greco-Roman civilization was its two-class society, the slave-class and the controlling oligarchic class. The slaves were lorded over by a lesser number of educated elitists who lived as parasites off the labors of the slave-class. Leisure and education were mainly the privilege of the oligarchy; control by the oligarchy was implemented by a rationale of not merely hierarchical legitimacy but also of its god-ordained necessity. Romanism includes the institutional politicizing of the Roman Empire and the underlying presumptions of class philosophy and theology, which in many aspects obtain even now in Western civilizations. If there is any doubt about the monumental impact of classical Greece and Rome on State and Federal Governments in the United States of America one needs only visit the U.S. Capitol, and indeed the various State Capitols. Greco-Roman architecture dominates government houses, both the insides and the outsides of legislative, judicial and executive *temples*.

Is Romanism failing? Yes, in two senses. In the sense that the slaver/slavee society is not sociably workable, politically, philosophically and theologically; and in the sense that the Romanist institutions now in place are in fact waning because of their incorporated, institutional injustices. The treatment of people as chattel, as so many treads on the ladder of hierarchical ascendancy, is not acceptable morally or practically.

The global cataclysms now pressuring all civilizations root in classicism. Romanism has become a colonial export to the nations of the world. In the course of the 20th Century, three main events occurred which have hastened the collapse of Romanism. The first two are World Wars I & II, and the third is the Second Vatican Council.

The underlying ferment in Europe that caused both wars was despotic European (Roman) nationalism, which for decades had been cannibalizing national, global economies. The despotisms of national tyrannies culminated in two widely destructive world wars; and their aftermath, the "cold war" and the eventual collapse of world Communism. While the wars' ultimate political effect was movement away from Romanist despotism, the mind of Romanism still persisted in Catholic theology—until the time of Vatican II. In effect and in clear language, Vatican II formally admitted the moral, ethical wrongs of failed Romanism, of the kind, which stridently motivated the spirit and intent of the Councils of Trent and the First Vatican. Their mind was (is) entrenched in the culture and politics of Romanism. These Councils implemented dogmatic strategies for the unvarnished purpose of confronting and defeating the Protestant

Reformation. The violent strategies of Counter-Reformationalism, including the Spanish and Roman Inquisitions, their justifications and twists of casuistry, were summarily thrown out the window opened by Pope John XXIII and The Second Vatican Council.

The exposure of inauthenticities enmeshed in gratuitous philosophical and theological presumptions, whether in political or religious institutions, inevitably gives impetus to their failures. The decade of the 1960s exploded in turbulent rebellion (Woodstock) against many of the Western world's institutions. The fixations of static theology also continue to quake since that time.

Jesus Christ stood up against institutional Romanism and got killed for it. Nevertheless, institutional Catholicism evolved hierarchies after the Roman model, notwithstanding that Jesus tried to get Peter to scratch from his mind any and all political schemes of kingdom-building. To argue the proposition that institutional Catholicism as it exists today corresponds to Jesus' work of messiahship, on its face, stretches credibility. Jesus' preferential option for the poor was a choice that avoided institutional fixation. His word and his example are calculated to spread as heart-to-heart leaven and to effect in human hearts motivations of love for one another. In this spiritual strategy of "symbiotic contagion" Jesus affirms the primacy scripture of paradigmatic nature.

It might be well for us to ask, "What is the point of this?" The point is: that we individually and as a nation are at the threshold of critical choice—the same choice confronting Jesus after his forty-day fast in the desert. One choice before him was to join the cultural class of Roman Judea's oligarchy (temple/political/business structure) and pursue positions of prestige, authority, and control over resources and others. Another choice was to go the other way and choose a future that would identify with the poor and the outcasts, with the slave class, and work to bring about a more equitable social structure. The latter, as we know, is the choice Jesus made, and it is the choice he asks of us too if we would claim to be his followers.

In his choice, Jesus categorically rejected the institutional culture of the Roman Empire. Romanism—empire-building—would not be an option for his true followers. But even his twelve, and especially, Peter, whom he chose to be leader, couldn't grasp Jesus' radically different messiahship. To understand Romanism, is to understand what we as "Church" are called not to be and not to do if we would be identified as "Christians."

The reality is that the institutional Catholic Church of today is even now infected with a mentality of imperial Romanism (in the institution of an elitist male hierarchy) that presumes itself to be exclusively God-ordained to "dispense the economy of grace." In its institutional description of purpose it uses commercial terminology as if God's grace were a marketable commodity.

Church mercantilism is patently fixated in the hierarchical structure, which purports to "market" grace on behalf of God to grace-lacking humans.

Individually, like Jesus, each of us must stand on the threshold of deciding which value-system we choose to be identified with. Will we choose to be dominators, comptrollers of commodities, and enslavers, or people of love who labor in the company of the enslaved in order to effect a more just society which responds to the moral imperative of seeing every person in equal standing before God and man, with right of equal access to life's necessities?

We should consider the nature of the "divine dispensation of grace" in paradigmatic nature. Throughout virtually the whole history of the evolution of life, it is the experience of life that every minutest component of life's web is born from, is sustained in, and returns to the economy of life's essential continuity. Only in the thinnest skin of recent history have self-conscious humans departed from this essential economy and presumed for themselves the libertarian arrogance of ignoring nature's time-proven strategy by choosing to exploit the rest of network life for self-advantage and without consideration for the consequences to other life and their own future.

The lessons of "Primary Scripture," the informed interpretation of God's natural word, are in our time quintessentially urgent if we would rise above the self-destructive misdirection of institutionalized Romanism. One way or another we "stir the pot"; the ingredients going in it are of our doing, as is the "spirit" coming from it. The discernment of spirits happens authentically in the process of reason; and, civility, the trimorphic resonance of faith/hope/love edifies civilizational tranquility. The opportunity for world peace is before us.

To borrow this thought from the Bard:
"Oh the webs that we humans weave."

Our ignorance and arrogance are but thieving
Spiders airing about their snares to entangle
All that approaches them; and unless we daily
Undo the enticements of their sticky strands
We also become mortally tangled cocoons,
So many dangling flies providently and duly
Staged to be consumed by our mini selves.
Our selves weave their own imprisoning cocoons,
Umbilicaled fetters of guilt and fear, codependent,
Ego-threatening traps of ignorance and arrogance.
Fear is nature's instinctive response to ignorance.
Guilt is truth-sense questioning egoism's arrogance.

TRANSUBSTANTIAL DIVINITY

Bread from Earth. Live grain.
Green flesh. Blue sunlight.
Cracked sugar. Sweet bread.
Sweet flesh. Broken.
Washed in sunlight.
Rainbow animated.
Celebrated water. Earth dust.
Raised carbohydrate consciousness.
Bread. Wine. Blood.
Body. Birth. Death.
Faith-deserving certainties.
Common continuities.
Grapeyness. True blue.
Fired steel. Color of soul.
Music of the spheres.
Darkness of deep oceans.
Sweating tectonic seams.
Bubbling transformation.
Red hot magma veins.
Spiritual ferment.
Juice changed to wine.
Wine to blood.
Blues songs.
True blue. True drink.
Truth in fragile skins.
Color purple.
Royal crowned Earth mortality.

RELATIVITY'S IMPERATIVE:
Life is a tide of rising consciousness;
Consciousness accommodates well-being;
Well-being is moral conscience, religion's soul;
Soul, religious conscience, is relativity's imperative.

Relativity & Religion

The dance of reason and faith. The advances of the physical sciences are astounding and intimidating to most of us. Yet we who are called to be teachers, whether as parents or ministers, owe it to our own authenticity and to those who come after us not to be fearful of new learning, even if it is complex, but rather to do our very best to understand it and to reconcile it with the cumulus of all prior learning ("science" in its philosophical, root meaning). To do less, in the least, is not to be good examples to children; at worst, it is to breach trust.

St. John tells us, "In the beginning was the Word, and the Word was with God, and the Word was God." The Word, as metaphor for God, tells us that above all else God communicates. God communicates in and through creation, which is the First Scripture, and in the written words expressing human consciousness, the Second Scripture. The-Word-Made-Flesh, Jesus Christ, is in Christian faith the link between divine and human communication / consciousness / conscience. Through communication and consciousness, we come to a self-awareness of our divine/human calling to conscience: love's rationality.

A caption to a figure depicting Christ's suffering says: "A common flaw among some Catholics is emphasizing the divinity of Jesus while denying his full humanity." (THE WITNESS, Dubuque, Iowa, Archdiocesan periodical, pg 1, 8/29/99.) Arguably, this flaw, through history, also has been a factor behind traditional Christianity's disconnection of the "supernatural" (spiritual) from the natural (material), and the resulting misdirection of the mass public.

When communication is transparently truthful, faith in the Word is secured. When this security is reached, human hope dares to be openly trustful of future transformations yet to be wrought by the Word. When this openness arises, consciousness can grasp the meaning of good and evil, know the difference, and freely choose the rational option of the greater good: the option of love. Personal commitment to the good, that which serves greater well-being, is the motive of love and of service in "priesthood"—to which all are called.

Nature is the paradigm and wisdom (i.e., text and context) upon which authentic religion advances. The quantum-electric universe is our present-day insight into the Creator's working of the Word. The theological truism has it that "grace supposes nature," and we might add that nature supposes grace. Either way, grace is effectively qualified by our understanding, or misunderstanding, of natural working. When we neglect Jesus' humanity and exaggerate his divinity, when we misperceive and misrepresent the unity of the supernatural and the natural, we deceive ourselves and mistakenly rationalize a worldview that does not correspond with reality. Mistakenly premised religion is destined to be found undeserving of belief. This is the present predicament confronting the fixations of Christian theology.

"Religious" communication is no less obligated than "scientific" communication to develop and use a vocabulary that is contemporary and accurate if it would teach "truth." All "relativity" is rooted in the essential substantiation of all matter, that is, in its transformative, quantum-electric materiality. This term shouldn't be intimidating to us, even if it is a description of elemental atomic substance. (The word "quantum" simply means a *something*, whether a subatomic particle, an atomic nucleus, an electron, or a planet or human body—the latter merely being complex assemblies of the former.)

The quantum-electric atom is the substance of every molecule—the energy and symmetry of all life. Atoms of all elements have two main components, the "nucleus," held together by a strong force (positively charged), and electrons (negatively charged) circling around the nucleus in a closely defined "sky" (and/or layered skies) depending upon the kind of element. Elements vary in their nuclear weights and electron numbers. The "gravity" attraction of the nucleus limits the freedom of electrons; electrons in the atom's outermost sky are less energetically tethered by the nucleus and are more freely given up or shared with other atoms or molecules. (A molecule is an assembly of one or more atoms; for example, a molecule of water is made up of one oxygen atom and two hydrogen atoms.)

The electron is a complex universal mechanism of elemental communication, and of all communication. All communication is quantum-electric. The potential for communication is a function of the electron fields of atoms and molecules. At each step of "communication," of electron sharing, a new outcome results; the new outcome has potentials altogether different from those of the contributing atoms/molecules. The elemental alphabet is atomic— electrons are letters—whose universal script/voice/word (i.e., arrangement) is molecular.

The sustaining synergy of the quantum-electric universe is energy-in-common that is "spiritually" informative. No matter how complex a molecule might be (even the human body), its word/work is quantum-electric. The "work" (nature or structure) is *body* whose "word" agency (nurture or energy) is *soul*. In the language of Sacrament, the *body* is the "sign" and the *word* is "grace"—the inspiration and expression of soul. In celebrating ritual Sacrament, except we also associate the natural sign with its nurtural grace, we fragment and misconstrue the holistic character (natural/supernatural) of Universal Sacrament. Informed consciousness demands that we keep "holy things" (*sacra*) in grateful "remembrance" (meminisse, *mentum*) for they come to us gratuitously and are to be engaged in/by us in trust.

If there is anything in nature that is prior to and even more universal to life than water, it is the cosmic ocean of subatomic energy operative in the whole universe. Without the subatomic, baptismal water doesn't exist. Electricity, which is of universal importance to human living, is the controlled channeling of electrons into all manner of usages. Photons are components of the electron-mix, and are agents of transformation.

The term "relativity" comes from Albert Einstein's two quantum-electric theories: 1) his "*Theory of General Relativity*" states that the gravity (mass potential) of bodies acts upon each other, and 2) his "*Theory of Special Relativity*" states the equivalency (interchangeability) of energy and mass, thus, his famous equation, $E=mc^2$, where E is energy (cosmic, thermodynamic), m is the mass of a body, and c^2 is the speed of light, squared.

"Soul" may be thought of as the energy potential of a quantum; the neural processing of vital (animal and human) activity. For example, thinking and communicating are thermodynamic processes. "Relativity" speaks to the interactivities of energy and substance with each other and is not to be confused with "relativism," a label for a too-common viewpoint, which equates "truth" with the self-advantaging whim of personal judgment independent of social implication. Conscience valuates judgment in terms of consequences to common well-being, whereas, circumstantial whim prioritizes personal convenience. Relativism is self-infatuation and ego idolatry.

Christian theology's crisis today might be stated as a crisis of credibility; so long as theological extrapolations in matters of nature and Earth/human relationships conflict with human experience, the credibility of theology is at issue. Therefore, until the universal, transformational/centering paradigm replaces the static/centrist paradigm of Christian theology, theological credibility will continue to be discredited. Historically cultured staticism and dualism, dogmatized in practice, are now imprinted factors in the sacrilege of Nature.

The "theological" hyper-fictionalizing of the "place" of heaven (its physical locus) has worked to the disadvantage of public respect for religion. We need to take seriously the radical truth of Pope John Paul II's words that heaven is not a "place in the clouds" but rather a "relationship with God." A deeper insight into the "scripture" of the universe informs respectful relationship; thus, the case for replacing in religion its static-centrist worldview with the transformational. Until this quantum leap in theology is made, the dead-end conundrum frustrating religious conscience and civility will yet remain.

The Economy of Grace

Salvation by word/work. The Catholic/Lutheran accord in the matter of salvation by faith and by good works is at the heart of common understandings of sacrament—the natural transformation of the quantum-electric universe. The "word" embodied in the *working* of the cosmos is encoded in the continuum of quantum-electric transformations. The transformational working of life's continuity is script in genetic codes inside every cell. The product of ongoing genetic composition is by way of the "spiritual" effort (bodily conscious energy) researching all the open possibilities of the encoded word, and by the application of consciousness in scripting new word associations that effect purposeful transformations.

The conscious power of "soul," inhering essentially in matter's structure, is the power of transformation, the "nurtural" component of life that encodes "sacred purpose" (sacra mens) in the quantum-electric unfolding/infolding of Earthlife's essential continuity.

Human consciousness is a foremost consciousness now impacting all Earthlife. Thus, we human beings, at this stage of Earthlife transformation, are "soul-power," for good or for ill, affecting Earthlife relationships. "Ex opere operato," that is, by the natural power of the inherency of essential continuity, natural law drives vital transformations, but, "ex opere operantis," that is, by the agency of personal intention and action (conscience), we engage intentionally the laws of transformational redundancy and reinforce nature's continuity codes and her sustainable well-being. Informed conscience confirms Nature, but, living unsustainably (uninformed) sacrileges Nature. The authenticity defining the transformational codes of Nature are within Nature's quantum-electric continuity, of which we—not of our own doing—are essential components; it is the natural code of Word/Work that calls us to live sustainably—in harmony—with the vital necessities of codependency—and not exploitively. By such living we are "grace" to one another.

REASON FOR HOPE—CONSCIOUSNESS

Centering or Centrism?

Subsidiarity. Subsidiarity is the structural paradigm of cosmic continuity and, specifically, of Earthlife. Life originates at the cellular level in the expression of female/male sexuality; life's social structuring is edified in female/male trust. The trinitarian community of mother/father/child expresses in faith/hope/love trinitarian likeness.

The division and self-replication of cells, in mitosis as in meiosis, are "centering" processes, the basic agency of transformational life. Driven also by the opposing positive/negative charges of cellular polarity, the chromosomes amass within the cell at the equatorial plane where they duplicate and where the cell splits to form two identical cells. And, on and on goes cell division wherein genetic messaging self-reprints over and over again in each and every new cell and regulates the individual development. The conception of the child occurs at the cellular level with the first joining of male/female germ cells; activated by the new genetic (parental) mix, the new cell (zygote) self-replicates, begins the new formation of the individual, and programs the division and differentiation of cells throughout the lifetime and until the death of the individual when the body cells molecularly disintegrate and give up their contents.

The universe, in the general scientific perception, is a quantum-electric complexity of interactive force fields, all of which are resourced in the original Big Bang. Before the Big Bang, a collapse state of "centrism" existed; after the Big Bang, "centering" became the organizational dynamic of energy/matter substantiation. All mass is particulate substantiation amassed in quantum-electric force fields. Centrism, also in human affairs, is an energy-collapse condition, whereas, centering is the constructive disposition of positively/negatively charged energies. The cosmic process of centering is universally operative according to time/space qualifications; these qualifications allow for the ongoing interactive diversifications of energy/matter. Thus, centering is understood to be a cosmic process of "subsidiarity," whose ongoing qualifications are a continuity of ongoing transformations. As such, it is the authentic paradigm for modeling social relationships. Subsidiarity is nature's problem-solving process that deals with the ad hoc entities involved in the "problem," which, generally, alone can ultimately act in their own interest. The principle of subsidiarity should be operative in human relationships, whether they are political, religious, whatever. Monarchical structures of church and state are inauthentic when they intervene the natural social working of subsidiarity in human affairs.

In principle, but too generally not in practice, the Roman Catholic Church endorses the principle of subsidiarity. But, today there are still strongly centrist ecclesiastical powers, which adamantly advocate for Rome's control over matters of personal conscience. This authoritarian overreaching isn't just frustrating to personal integrity/authenticity, it also defeats essential subsidiarity and damages the Church and all of humankind.

In the present context, what is an appropriate definition of subsidiarity? *Subsidiarity is a leadership process of shared decision-making and action-taking, based on the "jurisdictional" (right of voice) authenticity of every person by reason of birth.* The qualities of authenticity/integrity originate in the organic nature of subsidiarity. Laws of interpersonal relationships are authentic, integral, when they enable subjects mutually to elaborate essential personal/social well-being. Subsidiarity, the step-by-step substantiation of all subjectivity, is, as qualified by the physical laws of nature, quantum-electric. Quantum-electric subsidiarity is the cosmic paradigm of all vitality, including the institutional structure/function of religion/civility. In the quantum-electric assembly of organisms, their spiritual function (conscious intentionality) is characterized by and characterizes their personal/communal physicality.

Integrity, the wholeness of vital character, like subsidiarity, is instituted in the essential continuity (function/structure) of psychical/physical substantiation. The vital function of any organism depends on the "operational integrity" (Ladislas Orsy, "The Papacy for an Ecumenical Age," AMERICA, a Jesuit magazine, October 21, 2000, Vol. 183, No. 12, Whole No. 4503, pp 9-15) of its composing members (cells). Integrity is a state/outcome of functional subsidiarity. The epistle of St Paul to the Ephesians on the "mystical body" is really a treatise on subsidiarity.

Because of radically opposing viewpoints within the Roman Catholic hierarchy about subsidiarity and leadership roles, namely, whether participation by bishops in leadership is merely consultative (Vatican I viewpoint) or decision-making (Vatican II viewpoint), there is a real war for the control of the peoples' allegiances. The mind of Vatican II with respect to the leadership role of bishops is "collegiality," that is, *participative* input, not just *advisory. Collegial* ("col lege" is from the Latin *cum lege*; in compound words the prefix *cum* is sometimes transposed to *col*) also has the meaning of participation in keeping "with law," that is, inclusive of the rationality possessed as a gift by right of birth in every human being.

In his campaign to suppress Liberation Theology—Base Community Church built on the principle of subsidiarity—Pope John Paul II repeatedly exercised a bias in appointing bishops who interpret subsidiarity leadership as merely an advisory deference and not a participatory right. His recent raising of Pope Pius

IX (the pope of Vatican I) to sainthood, even though there was little public sentiment in support of it, is hard evidence of John Paul II's bias.

The conflicted leadership of the Roman Catholic Church has become such a public scandal as to be a factor in the laity's overall frustration and the decline of church attendance. The predicament that priests find themselves in because of the leadership turmoil is especially sad and tragic. Dishonesty, pretense, especially when practiced by church leadership, whether intentional or unintentional, vitiates faith and infects with distrust.

Joseph Campbell, an authority on the theologies of world mythologies, has quite well given perspective to the threat of centrist theology/religion:

"Are modern civilizations to remain spiritually locked from each other in their local notions of the sense of general tradition, or can we now break through to some more profoundly based point and counterpoint of human understanding?

"...[Al] though many who bow with closed eyes in the sanctuaries of their own tradition rationally scrutinize and disqualify the sacraments of others, an honest comparison immediately reveals that all have been built from one fund of mythological motifs, variously selected, organized, interpreted and ritualized according to local need, but, revered by every people on earth.

"...For it is a fact that the myths of our several cultures work upon us, whether consciously or unconsciously, as energy-releasing, life-motivating and directing agents, so that even though our rational minds may be in agreement, the myths by which we are living, or by which our fathers lived, can be driving us, at that moment, diametrically apart."

Except religion (church) authenticates the personal and social participation of every human being in the secular venue and in harmony with Nature's paradigm, it is misdirective; except religion corrects its exposed misdirection, it is dishonest.

The "People of God," as Church, "qua ecclesia," is the good news of Vatican II. Not a self-empowered hierarchy, but the subsidiary graces of God's People is the power of Church. The global peoples are "God's People."

Over time, the professionals of institutionalized churches have spawned an incestuous rationality that neither respects nor accepts the ideas of the laity. Thus, by their calculated consideration only of ideas coming from institutionally inbred sources, church professionals deprive the church of valid and enriching inputs that are uninfected by insider prejudice, and in so doing, church insiders excommunicate themselves from authentic sources that might free them from their myopia and allow them to escape the deadly troika of hierarchical centrism, exclusionism and irrelevance. While the laity may discern the destructive influences of these institutional biases, church hierarchy seems blind to them and/or to deny them, thereby being unfaithful to the public trust and preventing the grace of the laity to work for the good of all.

Cardinal Pierre Eyt of Bordeaux, France, member of the Curia and the Vatican Congregation for the Doctrine of Faith challenges curial unresponsiveness to lay ideas ("Prelate urges openness," The WITNESS, Dubuque, Iowa, Archdiocesan weekly periodical, pg. 9, 2/13/00):

"...The modern age is motivated by 'a profound evolution of moral and juridical conscience.' [The Cardinal asks] 'Couldn't this evolution bring us something new and clearer, something that would present itself in a rationality other than that of antiquity and that of the Middle Ages?'

"...In the profound examination of these subjects (doctrinal and pastoral difficulties involving church authority and the Catholic faithful) the church's reflection cannot end with an evocation of an ever-questionable Golden Age.

"...Cardinal Eyt said the church's current dialogue with the faithful generally comes to an abrupt end when it comes time to draw 'institutional conclusions' from the reflection. The church seems to 'mark time without going beyond the initial question...only rarely do our conclusions satisfy our partners. The least one could say is that they do not see the rationality and truth of these conclusions.'

" '...all these problems (relating to the synthesis between reason, faith and life) are linked and of equal gravity. They are interrelated. They belong to an indivisible whole.

"Cardinal Eyt also stated, 'whether one is a residential bishop or a cardinal of the Curia, law and decisions, judgments required of institutions cannot be delayed or procrastinated. Those in charge have their backs to the wall. While theoretical debate may be lacking in clarity practical decisions must be taken promptly.'

"While today's Catholics have ideas to contribute on questions of theology, politics, bioethics and other issues, the hierarchy's dialogue with them seems to be going nowhere."

Archbishop Guiseppe Pittau, Secretary of the Vatican Congregation for Catholic Education made comments along the lines of those of Cardinal Eyt ("Laity, key to education," id, pg, 2, 2/13/00):
"The influential Catholic core should be formed by first-rate intellectuals who have reached a certain synthesis between their academic discipline and their Catholic faith.

"...The United States is probably the only place (where) you can have a theological conversation with lay people.
"...Communion needs communication to grow and communication is the means to solving many problems at the starting point.

"...the bishop should not feel uncomfortable in calling the (College) president for an exchange of views of one of the most important apostolates in his diocese, the intellectual apostolate of the dialogue between faith and reason and culture."

Some professionals within the Catholic Church have recognized the seriousness of the problem of the isolation of church leadership from the laity:
"One of the most serious issues facing the church today may be the isolation of the ordained ministers from a solidarity with the laity which would allow them to stand in their midst as persons with credentials to speak authoritatively. Just as the problems of each culture and historical epoch differ, so will the manner in which leadership will be exercised; so, too, must indigenous culture, history and sociology affect the shape of the church's corps of ordained ministers." (1)

Other professionals outside the churches recognize the essential resource that lay people are to general societal advancement in its many facets of professional interest:
"Since policies concerning the human environment require both social judgment and specialized scientific knowledge, perceptive and informed laymen can often contribute as much as technical experts to their formulation. In certain cases, indeed, lay men may be wiser judges than experts because their overall view of the complexity of human and environmental problems is not distorted by the parochialism which commonly results from technical specialization." (2)

"Personally, I make a special effort to pay frequent visits to the small universities and colleges of the Midwest. And I'm impressed by the number of young people who are very open-minded and who will certainly come up with the most original, the most unexpected ideas. When you go to Harvard or the Rockefeller University you find admirable people, but they've already started down one path and are not likely to leave it. So I'm rather glad when someone risks wasting a little money by giving it to a young professor at the University of Clermont-Ferrand, because there are certainly lots of young people there who haven't yet become part of the establishment's way of thinking and who can do something new." (3)

As long as the institutions of society alienate themselves from each other in a self-induced myopia of arrogance, egoism will continue to work its havoc in civilizations. The impregnation of societal institutions with the seminal richness of open and interactive dialogue may activate in civilizations a new wisdom, a new flowering of harmonious living, and in individuals a "new phylum" of consciousness characterized by the conscionable motives of trust, responsibility and love for one another and all life on Earth.

1. New Ministries, William R. Burrows, Orbis Books, Maryknoll, N.Y, 1980
2. Only One Earth, The Care & Maintenance of a Small Planet. Ward & Dubos, Report on the Human Environment, Inc., W.W. Norton & Company, Inc., N.Y., 1972, Preface, pg. xvii.
3. Quest, Reflections on Medicine, Science, and Humanity, Dubos & Escande, Harcourt Brace Jovanovich, Inc., N.Y., 1980, pg. 29.

Quantum Leap

The New Phylum: the phylum of love. Jesus' coming marks a break with patriarchism harshly habituated in instinctual consciousness—the "old law." He recognized that human living according to the law of the jungle—an eye for an eye, and a tooth for a tooth—is not acceptable for humankind if the graces of living by faith, hope and love are ever to be fully experienced. The law Jesus gave is to "love God with your whole heart, your whole soul, your whole mind and all your strength, and your self and your neighbor as yourself." In this mandate Jesus lays the ground for a quantum shift away from fear, guilt, domination, violence and self-advantaging, to a new consciousness of love's human/divine potential.

Prior to Jesus' time the potential of the "divine" in human consciousness was little understood and even less pursued. God was experienced externally, not internally as the voice of inner consciousness. The message Jesus leaves for all people of all time is that "by your love for one another" divinity is possessed in you and witnessed to others—the same love that Jesus received from his Father. When we follow this maxim of Jesus, he claims us to be his own—Jesuits—and he enables us to rise from jungle consciousness to a new phylum of consciousness.

Teilhard de Chardin recognized, unlike most before him and after him until now, the natural evolutionary *necessity* of becoming "a people of love" by the natural, cosmic process of transformational consciousness. In integrating theology and "scientia," and in the context of transformational rationality (self-aware energy), Chardin called for a quantum leap in consciousness, as did Jesus' before him, namely, to live by conscience and by love's awareness of universal, transcendent salvation. From his perspective of scientific awareness he recognized that the collective result of such living would raise humankind to a heretofore unachieved status of consciousness, namely, to a new "phylum of love."

When parents upgrade their personal consciousness and their family-devotion to the rationality of love they will empower their children in love, and when love becomes imprinted in the family-living code a new phylum of love will come to be. Biologically, we can become then, collectively, in fact, a new phylum of love; then can love become the distinguishing character of our relationships with all other life; then can ontogeny recapitulate a new phylogeny, a new genetic code and a new era of peaceful determination to give place to and bring harmony to all life on Earth.

We are called to make a quantum leap into a new dimension—the dimension of love. We are called to rise above the mere (fight-flight) instincts of the avian-reptilian brain to the conscious intuitions of the cortical brain. Altruistic individuality, redundantly imprinted in the social psyche, can characterize a new sociality. "Soul" in micro-quanta can characterize new soul in amassed macro-quanta. The birth of new life is a resurrection occurrence, a continuity process of soul/substance arising out of prior spirituality/materiality. The ascent into the conscious world of personal responsibility is ascent into the new phylum of love. *This is the new dispensation*: that rational judgment is empowered to make conscious decisions of choice and override the hard imprint of script necessity (instinct). However, if we mindlessly disregard the hard imprint, which has been script to a good purpose, it is to our own peril. It is there for us to use for our own and for Earthlife's common advantage, thus, instinct needs to be factored into any choices that would go against it. Conscious judgments like instincts need to be made from the viewpoints of the individual as well as the communal good.

Instincts as well as conscious judgments sometimes require that the communal good and the safeguarding of others be given priority over personal good. Even at peril to one's personal life. There is no greater gift than that one lays down his/her life for another. Such choice is the Christian choice. Such lived, personal commitment is what the Christian life is about; by it we identify with Jesus and are recognized as God-conformed. So let it happen. Either we do it together or we all struggle in a purgatory aggravated by egoistic doing/undoing.

PUZZLING REFLECTION
The waveless sea reflects faithfully
The fullsome sun.
But choppy seas are shimmering tinsel,
Crinkled sunshine.
So it is with introspection.
Reflective reason shows whole
Awareness of unity Sacrament
In the word/work of faith, hope, and love.
The crinkling of nerve calm reflection
Distracks the trains of thought.
Reason and faith are parallel rails,
The Alpha way to Omega destiny,
Beginning with communication
And ending in love.

SYNONYMS.
Live and learn.
Except one learns
One doesn't live.

Theology Renewed

Teilhardiana. In the first half of the 20th Century institutional Roman Catholicism was glorying in the perceived successes of its counter-reformational offensive. In this timeframe the Church achieved the implementation of its Tridentine will, confirmed and expanded by Vatican I, namely, of clerical electionism and exclusionism. Perhaps the Church's peak moments of triumphalism were realized in Pope Pius IXth's excommunication of modernism (1864), and in the canonization (1931, by Pius XI) of Robert Bellarmine, S.J., the chief theologian of the Roman Inquisition (1600), which condemned the theologian/philosopher Giordano Bruno and the scientist Galileo Galilei.

Against this backdrop of strident triumphalism priest/scientist Pierre Teilhard de Chardin, S.J., appeared on the Church scene. His appearance was not well received by official Church. Since the time of Bruno and Galileo a tensioned compromise had been struck between Church (theology) and science (philosophy), namely, the separation of proprietary turfs into the realms of the spiritual and the material, and the understanding that Church would rule in matters theological (spiritual), and science would keep itself to things material. Chardin, to the chagrin of both, was a meddler in this tidy arrangement that artificially cleaved truths of science from those of theology. To him this schism must have seemed a violation of truth's unity and of commonsense logic. His understandings of truth's unity would do nothing less than sow the seeds that would unravel publicly the schism of convenience forged by the mutual distrust of religion and science.

Given the harsh and absolutist mindset of his Church against new science, Chardin had good reason to worry about Church reaction against him. If Chardin responded by trying to walk a tightrope that would not offend either the truths of science or Church dogma, it is understandable. Given the constraints of the Church mind of the time, such endeavor now seems as folly for it was then and is now an impossibility. Since Vatican II things are changing for it is openly recognized that *"The human race has passed from a rather static concept of reality to a more dynamic, evolutionary one. In consequence, there has arisen a new series of problems, a series as important as can be, calling for new efforts of analysis and synthesis."* (Joseph Gremillion, The Gospel of Peace & Justice, Copyright 1976, Fifth Printing, March 1980, Page 247, Gaudium et Spes, Introductory Statement, No. 5, Para 4, Orbis Books, Maryknoll, N.Y. 10545). So, it is unfair to fault Chardin now for the mental gymnastics he exercised under the circumstances and to discredit his whole body of thought for its insufficiency. True enough, his reconciliation of science and religion may not be perfect, however, advances in science and theology today afford the opportunity to advance a more perfected reconciliation of science and religion. Teilhard made a good and useful beginning.

The word "teilhardiana" means here understandings of theological insight resourced in quantum-electric transformations, as, in a manner, anticipated in Chardin's thought and writing. In keeping with St. Anselm's maxim, "faith searching intelligence," Teilhard's religious/intellectual writings seek to flesh-out the compatibilities of belief/knowledge. Because of the faith constraints put on intelligibility and rationality, the reconciliation of religion/science is a continuing and urgent endeavor. For example, we might consider, in the light of quantum-electric science, fundamental theological terms, such as "transubstantiation."

A theology of cosmic continuity might understand transubstantiation as the continuity power of resurrection (birth-faith), of ascendance (consciousness-hope) and of transcendence (conscience-love). In the transubstantiation of the bread we eat and the wine we drink—the assimilation of "divine presence" in "eucharist"—our persons are daily edified in soul/substance, in spirit/matter. *Eucharistic* transubstantiation is essential soul/body nourishment, which we commemorate in the Mass, the ritual memorial of Jesus' last meal.

If we would understand the natural meaning of transubstantiation (molecular disintegration/integration) we need to consider quantum-electricity, which substantiates conscious materiality. Quantum-electric transubstantiation occurs at the atomic/molecular level. Conventional chemistry views electrons as packaged "planets" (quanta) orbiting the atomic nucleus, much like Earth does the Sun. Electrons are perhaps better understood as "debris" fields energetically clouding atomic nuclei and interacting in the overlapping wavefields of molecules, like cloudy oyster-plasma enveloping the pearl. In the overlap and interpenetration of molecular debris fields, serendipity potentials (transubstancing) evolve by particulate interactivities constructing mass and perhaps also degrading into masslessness. A good example of such everyday serendipity, redundant and reliably predictable, are also the edifications occurring in and by green plant chlorophyll, namely, photosynthesis, the sunlight constructions of water and carbon-dioxide into carbohydrate (CHOH) networks, including those stored in live grain seeds. How impressive that the Prophet Isaiah presaged "eucharist" in his insight that "all flesh is grass"!

Another bit of conventional wisdom tells us that certain microorganisms, for example, those in the gut that are responsible for digesting and assimilating food, are obtained in a child from her/his mother in the fortuitous but external "infections" by the mother. Accidental infection seems not to be in character with natural redundancy and reliability. From the quantum-electric perspective it would seem probable that these agencies might originate physiologically from within the body's own cell systems as natural expressions of genetic codes. Organelles, the plastids and mitochondria, vital energy agencies, are themselves subtle symbiotic assemblages of onetime autonomous organisms now interdependently bonded and possessing their own DNA resourced in cell cytochrome rather than in the nucleus. As such, they are maternal in origin, that is, they are present only in the ovum and not in the sperm DNA, which enters the ovum. The retro-construction of organelle symbionts may be within the enzyme capabilities of cellular biology. (Retroviral infection, for example, HIV, involves the pirating and run-away usage by the infecting virus of the body's own genetic material; the retrovirus uniquely identifies with the infected body.) In light of these considerations, one might *theologically* reason that femaleness is vitality's groundstate, and that live cell processes (resurrection/ascendance/transcendence) are essentially female powers. The "Holy Spirit" agency in the Godhead seems rightly understood as a female agency of spirituality, as do faith, hope and love.

From the joined insights of theology and science we are opened to new understandings of essential female creativity, as it reflects on the Godhead, operating in creation. Wisdom is reason-built faith, the Mother Pearl, the ever open revelation of deity encoded in natural scripture.

"Christogenesis" is a transformational (ascendant/transcendent) process of consciousness *substantiated photosynthetically*. In recognizing that all flesh is a complexity of photosynthetic continuity, Isaias recognized that all flesh is one, one transubstantial Eucharist, one Sacrament, one Christogenetic Mystical Body.

New Meanings

Essential Chardin: theology in the quantum-electric universe. Evolution. The driven pace of cumulative ecological catastrophes (e.g., species and habitat destruction, globally spread industrial pollution) quickens the urgency of the search for a way out of humankind's dead-end determination. The persisting habit of Western societies in positioning science and religion (reason and faith) against each other makes them ineffective agencies in dealing with the mortal impasse. The French Jesuit, Pierre Teilhard de Chardin (1881-1955), is perhaps the first and surely the most systematic professional man of religion and science to deal seriously with their reconciliation in the common venue of human consciousness. But Chardin has suffered rejection from both camps, each for its own self-asserting reasons. It should be no surprise that Chardin's efforts to enlighten a new theology consistent with new science were thwarted by the status-quo dogmatists of his Church. In the absolutist tradition of Tridentine/Vatican I Catholicism, Roman Catholic officialdom especially eschews evolution, the basic premise of Chardin's "modernist" worldview. (However, Pope John Paul II now calls evolution "more than a theory.")

Chardin came to the unshakable belief that humankind could and would grow generationally (noogenesis) into an evolved (more perfected) consciousness of love (amorization). The reason-based consciousness of love would, as the effective motivator of personal action, raise humankind from its ego-centrist motivation to a new "phylum." Personal fullness ("pleroma"), as well as final realization (Omega) for the human phylum, is achieved in the personal/social embrace of the motive of love in all human conduct. The conscious choosing of the motive of love in all personal conduct can gradually raise humankind from a merely self-centered (biogenesis/anthropogenesis) evolution to a higher (divine) order of other-consciousness—Christogenesis. The present human phylum is entrapped by the instincts of ignorance, arrogance and egoism, the antitheses to faith, hope and love. This entrapment is a continuing legacy of deep-rooted fixations ("memes"—to use Richard Dawkin's word), fixations of patriarchism, centrism, sexism, staticism, chosenism and absolutism. The power of rationality, possessed by the cortical brain, is capable of raising human consciousness above the instinctive fixes of the avian-reptilian brain; the power of reason (evolutionary consciousness) is the trimorphic process of communication (faith), consciousness (hope) and conscience (love). Reason advances the power of purpose, which seeks and opts choices that serve the greater common good—which ultimately coincide to serve also the greater individual good. The choice of altruism, the tested choice of authentic reason, of common well-being, is the choice of "amorization." Reason and "true" faith converge into a mutually reinforcing consciousness/conscience; thus, faith and reason, rooted in and derived from common experiential consciousness, are not and cannot be in conflict; if they are in conflict it is because of misinformed rationality, fideism and/or willful obtuseness.

The lived Christian example is the lived expression of the virtues of the Trinitarian Godhead, which are, faith, hope and love. In Christian faith, divinity is seen to be present in the person of Jesus Christ, The "Second Person" of the Godhead. The "persons" of the Godhead are manifest in creation by natural virtues which give to natural transformation (evolution) its "inherent/coherent" virtues, that is, the purposefulness of evolution; thus, faith, hope and love are naturally expressed in the reasoned consciousness of the natural order, in the evolved continuity of cosmic relativity. The gift of faith is understood as a parental (first person) virtue; hope is associated with offspring (second person), and love is personified in the communication of parent/offspring. The ultimate, full term evolution of communication/consciousness/conscience is "Pleroma," the ultimate convergence of conscious creation into "Omega." Conscious Earth (self-aware life) is called to Godlikeness, to "second person" inheritance. At any point in time, the fullness attained by vitality in the process of evolution is a transformationally advanced state of "essential continuity," of cosmic relativity.

The evolution of symbioses in the trimorphic process of communication, consciousness and conscience, is the natural revelation of the divine in creation. Faith, hope and love, as the antitheses to the egocentric vices of ignorance, arrogance and greed, are also their antidote. The "phylum of love" cannot come to be except by the process of "amorization," a trimorphic continuity process of intentional transformation, of rationality coming to Light.

Convergence. Chardin speaks of "convergence," which has a correlative, divergence; their correlation, both in physical and theological terms, seems not to be well clarified. Perhaps by considering them in quantum-electric terms we may better understand their symmetry/energy, material/spiritual relativity. In space, vast deep space and molecular space, the cosmic looms weave, unweave and reweave. All space/time (subject/object/transformation) is qualified by electrical polarities, that is, by the atomic/molecular potential of negative/positive valencies. Particulate action around positive/negative poles is at the same time selectively attractive and repulsive, compositional and oppositional, which is to say, particles both converge and diverge.

The orbital movement of substances within the influential skies of bi-polar electricity may be elliptical as well as radial. Elliptically defined fields as well as spherical (global) may be established around strongly charged poles (as for example, the North and South Poles of Earth) with an energetically defined equator halfway between them. (In cellular bi-polarity, for example, the development of new life happens only when the ovum is fertilized; chromosomal division at the plane of the cell's equator cannot happen until fertilization.)

Bi-polar dynamics also vitalize the Earth "cell." Within the spheres of global activities convergence may eventually originate as the result of prior divergence. Electric polarity is a cosmic motor of many facets. Quantum-electric flux occurs at the Earth's opposing poles and "communicates" in solar space; the energy-flux at the poles establishes a generally elliptical space about the Earth with the Earth's two poles functioning as the foci of the elliptical region. The elliptical structure encapsulates the Earth within a life-supporting cocoon, a "sky," in Chardin's word, a "noosphere." The selective dynamic of electro-magnetic "conversation" qualifies substances in ways that give rise to new substances, to new sensitivities and to more subtle consciousness. By the processes of divergence/convergence, substance/consciousness evolves into refined and ever more diversified nerve-webs of communication. The harmonic attenuation of radiant energy by atoms and molecules intensifies the dynamics of molecular attraction/repulsion. We may understand this motor agency as nature's dynamism driving resurrection, ascendance and transcendence. This qualified *motor energy* is the natural agency of sacrament, of "Christogenesis," the intentionality of purposeful soul/substance evolved from intensional energy/matter.

Continuity. Cosmological dimension (MC^2) is at any point in time an essential continuity, the whole of space/time/energy/matter that connects back to the original Big Bang singularity; these are the four transformational dimensions of cosmic relativity, ever changing. Matter is transubstantial spirituality, that is, time-qualified, diversified spirituality. Materiality originates in and returns to spirituality. In the language of physics (Einstein's), energy (E) is unqualified spirituality, whereas, materiality (MC^2) is qualified spirituality, that is, light-substantiated mass. The origin of the universe is from unqualified, first singularity; at the Big Bang moment of cosmic unfolding, energy, spirituality, began its space/time, qualified/quantified unfolding. The qualification of spirituality, of energy into materiality, is a time-measured transformation, and, the quantification of substance is the spatial dimension of materialized qualification.

Materially/spiritually, the quantification/qualification of cosmic continuity advances by the trimorphic dialectic of communication, consciousness and conscience. Found in the self reflective awareness of the human person, the conscious product of the trimorphic dialectic, are the trimorphic virtues of faith, hope and love, the motivational agencies that qualify human judgment and decision-making. The altruism of these virtues represents the inherent good faith of cosmic dynamism itself. In religious parlance this dynamism is consciously sensed to be personal and purposeful; "God" is the named power of creative personality and intentionality. "Holy Spirit" is Sacred Intentionality inhering all substantiality. (It is notable that Scriptures call God "Light.") The purposeful advancement of the intentional virtues of faith, hope and love, evidences God-consciousness, as human consciousness apprehends it, and as such is a "divine" presence. The trimorphic presence (virtues) of divinity is advanced (or frustrated) by human intentionality and (in)action. To use Chardin's word, the advancement of divine virtue is "Christogenesis," the genesis of God-consciousness in flesh; God-conformed intentionality, functioning in human conduct, is the purposeful work (redemption) of divinity, the process of bringing conscious Earth to fullness (Pleroma) and gradual completeness (Omega) in God likeness.

Redemption. Chardin is sometimes faulted for inadequately considering in his theological scheme the Catholic teaching on redemption. Catholic theology bases the need for redemption on the Genesis account of humankind's "first" (original) sin. It must be remembered that the cosmic presumption underlying the original sin story and its evolved theology is belief in a stabilized, steady state universe that has Earth at its center. The creation account in Genesis reinforces this belief in its description of creation as happening by discretely separate and seemingly independent creative acts; in each creative act, what was created came "ex nihilo," that is, "from nothing." Theological habit in the course of the centuries was cultured to accept literally the Genesis Creation story. Literal creation is an insurmountable problem for Chardin and evolution, for the evolutionary worldview (quantum-electric) and the static-centrist worldview (Old Testament) differ fundamentally. The irreconcilability of the acentric-trans-formational worldview (represented by Bruno and Galileo) and the traditional centrist-static worldview put the institutional Church in such a crisis of faith that it felt compelled to deal harshly with the would-be innovators, i.e., by instituting the Spanish and Roman Inquisitions.

Though perhaps stated differently, it seems that Chardin's sense of "Christogenesis" includes humankind's (conscious Earth's) awakening to Earth's cosmic grace endowment for self-perfection, and to the conscionable obligation of self to commit to personal/social perfecting. The grace of "Christic" fulfillment (Pleroma) is accomplished by humans in the Christic living of faith, hope and love; the lived practice of these virtues (virtues owned in God/Christ) brings fullness not just to humans but to all interdependent Earthlife.

What seems apparently to be missing in the theological development of original sin is the role played by humans in their real violations of nature; it is real violations of nature that substantiate the awareness and the meaning of the "original" sin story. Humankind today, as always, is torn by conflicting biblical mandates, i.e., to "increase and multiply" and to refrain from consuming "the fruit of the tree in the middle." The "fruit" of the tree in the middle of the garden, the "Middletree," is a metaphor for the vital resourcefulness of Eden's (Earthlife's) sustaining network. Very obviously, the destruction of Earthlife's resourcefulness is a greater mortal threat to human existence today than it was in "Eden's" time. Experience in the Middle East, long before the story of the first sin was written, caused the people to suffer severely from the mortal waste of ecological greenery; populations warred then even as they do now for the meager fruits of their bioregion. Globally, we are ambiguously torn by our appetite for reproducing our own kind and by the mortal strain on Earth resources caused by prolix offspring.

Sin's resolution is in divine virtue made accessible in the grace of consciousness. All sin is ultimately a human failure to opt love's reason. Waste of nature tops the list. "Redemption" comes with the option of love. Redemption isn't just a spiritual consciousness; included in the need for redemption, first and foremost, is action to repair and respect ravaged Nature, the material/spiritual resource of all body/soul vitality. The embrace of love's motive (conscience), and the process by which love is achieved (communication-faith and consciousness-hope), need both to be affirmed in the natural (ecological) venue. Essential to the natural venue is the continued sustainability of network life's resourcefulness. Consumptive greed's wanton desecration of natural resourcefulness is ongoing "original sin." To the purpose of "redeeming" natural resourcefulness are "sabbath" and "jubilee"; the *sabbath* rest is needed for personal recovery, while jubilee forgiveness and ecological recuperation are needed to restore the overtaxed sustainability of people and Earth. Earth-fabric and human fabric need continuous repair; they cannot endure unrelenting exploitation.

Relativity. The continuum between Alpha and Omega sustains all being/becoming. In Chardin's word this continuum is "milieu," and in Einstein's equation it is MC^2. Relativity characterizes all the interdependencies of qualification/quantification, of energy/matter, of spirituality/materiality in the time/space continuum. Included in the meaning of Einstein's term MC^2 is the wholly substantiated quantum-electric cosmos as it exists at any moment in time. Earth and all life are transformational components of the quantum-electric cosmos. Personal fulfillment at any given moment in the transformational process is the fullness (Pleroma) of Omega up to that time. MC^2, the transformational cosmos, ever advances toward ultimate "Pleroma:Omega," toward evolutionary endstates and beginnings. Because naturally occurring contingencies cannot be predicted, neither can the endstates of Earth transformation. One important and unpredictable contingency, especially as far as network life is concerned, is the daily choices that humans make in interacting with network life. The fact is that all life on Earth is contingently interdependent (codependent in relativity). More than any other creature humans have the power to dominate and devastate all other contingent life, and therefore, to play a determinative role with respect to Earthlife evolution. The short-term and self-serving vision of humans is truly a catastrophic threat to the time-required evolutionary process of "biogenesis / anthropogenesis / Christogenesis," notwithstanding the fact that humans possess the consciousness-potential of understanding the immediate consequences of their actions and can opt choices of action that are more benign as to long term consequences. It is within the powers of human judgment to qualify human personality, choice-by-choice, and make people, individually and collectively, a "new phylum of love" wherein human conduct comes to be reasoned on terms of informed conscience/love. The Sacrament of life (holistic memory), subconsciously and consciously, is a cosmic agency of vital continuity.

Transfiguration. And how does the old phylum transform into the new? Earthlife evolution is a very specific form of cosmic transformation; in the specific, trimorphic resonance is its agency. Along its way evolution marks endings, but also beginnings, for each ending is a new beginning. Thus, in the course of evolution there are endstate (ecstatic) occurrences that presage new beginnings. The concentration of harmonic energies can excite molecular synergisms to such levels as to cause movement across a threshold into a new state; such an occurrence may be called "ecstatic resonance." The biblical account of the transfiguration of Jesus seems to describe just such an occurrence of resonant ecstasy. Jesus' expressed experience of being perfectly attuned to the will of his Father had such a glowing effect on him that it also overwhelmed his companions, Peter, James and John. Peter was so affected that he wanted to build monuments to the experience on the spot, monuments that also commemorated the ecstatic experiences of other prophets. We also experience something of the "transfiguration" ecstasy when we sense ourselves to be right with the world, with everybody and everything around us. (Heaven's beatific vision.) A jubilant sense of well-being resonates our every fiber. Ecstatic resonance births inspired insights. Harmonic resonance has a relative capacity for energy attenuation, which is transformationally effective. The quantum-electric potential for episodic energizing is a fact-basis of transformational relativity. (A physical example of ecstatic resonance is the shattering of glass crystal that occurs when the glass molecule is targeted with an energy-wave (sound) that matches its resonant frequency; also, the collapse of a suspension bridge when set to swaying by the wind. Attenuated resonant energy can reach a threshold, which triggers molecular transformation (electrical discharge). Another example of resonant ecstasy in biology is sexual orgasm.

Putting ourselves right with all things in every fiber of our soul/substance brings us as close to the experience of heaven as we can hope on Earth. Harmonic well-being isn't possible except we are tuned to network life's rhythms that vitalize also our own body molecule.

In order to envision Chardin's optimism in humanity's future as a "phylum of love," we need to contrast it with the pessimism of the human phylum preoccupied in consumptive egoism and prevalent in his day. The pessimistic human phylum is possessed with centrist memes of self-importance; it lives by hierarchical posturing, by rule making and enforcement.

The dominion arrogance of historied patriarchism obsesses even in property claim over women and children. This arbitrary, instinct-based habituation is self-idolizing centrism, which results in personal pessimism and obsessive self-consumption—the experience of hell. The compulsive competition of male hordes loosens mortally the bull in the china closet. Nihilism, emptiness, a present day disease, possesses the human psyche. The fraud of consumerist objectivism is radicalized in staticism, centrism and absolutism. These conspiratorial isms institute and justify ignorance and arrogance. The institution and justification of these are corporatized collectively by subsuming on behalf of corporations the civil rights of the individual person. The legal standing of the "corporate person" in law enables international business, free of personal risk, to exploit public resources globally. The delusions of patriarchal domination are enmeshed in the logic of multi-national corporatism, and the essential resources of peoples are prostituted by corporate greed. The sanctioned culture of corporate exploitation poisons individual conscience, which for self-advantage justifies interpersonal exploitation. Ego-centrism corporately corrupts values. The acculturated exploitation of people and natural resources—consumerism—is ethically endorsed in the *religious* mind of the community. The inauthenticity of exploitive consumerism establishes the commonplace vogue of distrust.

The political ratification in two-party politics of the adversary presumption pits individual against individual, corporations against individuals, and frustrates the Christian ethic. The church/state conspiracy in corporatized government, business and education works its fraud on nature and people. Jesus' mandate and Chardin's call for a "new phylum of love" challenge the consumerist presumptions of corporate feudalism, Hegel's and Rome's infallibilist theology of objectified statism—centrist and absolute.

Chardin's new phylum of love envisions a resurrection-future of liberation from all forms of self-obsessiveness. A person free of hard-wired memes (culture-based fixations) is a person who knows her own relativity and is infinitely thankful for the gift of gratuitous participation in providentially sustained Earthlife; such a person not merely tolerates but values diversification and delights in not wanting to possess more of Earth resourcefulness than what's needed for a self-fulfilled life; such a person is as zealous in facilitating others in coming to self-fulfilled living as she is for herself. Such people come to be recognized in their love for one another, in "Christogenesis."

COMMUNICATION is word correspondence; communion is the reciprocity of joined works; community is the diversification of mutuality. In their social resonance the expression of divinity—Trinity—is experienced. In their harmonic transformations, resurrection, ascendance, and transcendence are the social experience of symbiosis—sacrament. In communication faith resurrects essential openness in other-seeking; in communion hope ascends within consciousness reciprocal mutuality; and in community (self-giving) love transcends (serves) the diversification of other.

What is the task of theology in the quantum-electric universe? The task of theology is to explicate the enduring significance of the quantum-electric nature of all soul/substance, from its elemental, sub-atomic state to its highest awareness in molecular complexity. And, the role of science? To inform consciousness at all levels in its essential interdependencies. Science and religion are the conjoined consciousness of The Self's word/work.

HEAVEN'S DIVERSITY
The many rooms in my family home
Bid the occupants
Not to dwell too long in any one
But to transition,
From the persona aired in one, to another,
And then to become there
Accommodated in the space-charged atmosphere.

THE PRIDE OF " ISMS"
An "Ism" is a Lucifer, a short-lived star,
Whose sparks start conflagrations;
Dying, he leaves in his arc, darkness.
"As a mad Lion he rages in search
Of whom he may devour." (First Peter 5:8)

The atomic core's great force
Discovered in Modernism
Is stalked by clouds of weak force Isms.
But, as a scientific, philosophic and theologic
Force, the advance of Modernity
Will not be stayed
Even as the debris fields, electrons,
Negatively agitated at the core,
Cannot be denied their power to transform.

Empiricism is the trial-and-error Photon
Advocating for Chaos his contributions;
Rationalism, synergized Chaos,
Notwithstanding Absolutism's taboos,
Will perseveringly expose Fideism.
Though Relativism pleads a greater role
For the morality of voodoo Egoism,
Literalism's evidence of consequences,
Confronts him at the bar of Justice.
Materialism must realize that he could not
Make his own case except for Spiritualism;
Their half-truths together
Might come close to satisfying
Truth's judgment.

Though the 10-lion Pride for now
May be scattered, it will
Almost certainly reappear hungry
And clothed in new cloth.
The pride-demons are the same,
Though their appearances change
From time to time. Joined in religious
Logic to dominate are Elitism,
Judgmentalism, Authoritarianism.

Sylvester L. Steffen

Triumphalism.
But there is one Lion King over all
Whose jungle law is Monarchism, and
Whose roar intimidates all egos
In their personal, compulsive obsessions.
His name is Patriarchism;
His stomach is Consumerism,
His appetite so huge
His immorality is omnivorous.
He devours everything at will.
He is sexually hyper-serviceable.
Closer than he knows is this Patriarch
To crossing over the threshold
To spontaneous self-consumption.
Patriarchism's Consumerism
Is blasphemy, self-idolatry's
Absolute passion for waste.
This Lucifer's kingdom
Is a burned-out waste land.
Not even the good escape the Pride
Of excessive self-assertion,
The root of evil's aggression.
Before Mortal Sin can be stopped
He must be identified.
"Sobrii estote et vigilate!" (First Peter 5:8)
(Keep your wits about you and look out!)

ON THE OTHER SIDE
In our lifetimes we can't avoid being pelted with pesky little stones
As we sojourn; but we can join life's continuum of cobblestones
Into an aggregated roadbed. Milestones marked,
I've built a mile long bridge spanning the chasm
Separating the material from the spiritual,
And I have crossed to the other side only to discover
That both reside on both sides of the divide.

So I have returned to the original material side
Knowing that its soul like mine is spiritual too.
My lifetime effort continues to secure the mile long bridge
So others who come along can more easily negotiate the divide
And discover the soul/substance of common existence.
My self is no longer agitated by the artificial schism
For I am now, after bridging the division, conscious
Of essential continuity, also, on the other side.

Electrical Spirituality

The energy of transformation. "Quantum relativity" is an energy phenomenon of particulate interaction, of cosmic energy. All subatomic-atomic energy, physical and psychical, is of a common genre, that is, a phenomenon of *electron excitement* (electricity). Chardin recognized "human energy" as a subtle complexification of cosmic energy, but he approached the subject with great sensitivity for he was aware that it may challenge the traditional belief of soul/body disconnection and the Church-advanced belief in adversarial relationship between spirituality and materiality, between soul and body. Studies of human psychology confirm the role of electrons in neural messaging. Brain cites literally "light up" when electrons fire in the course of brain activities. Electrons are messengers of consciousness.

Electron excitement (electricity), as we know from daily experience, is a harnessable form of quantum-electric energy. The relativity of positive/negative charges is characteristic of quanta (protons and electrons). The protons in the atomic nucleus are positively charged, while the electrons traveling in the "sky" (wavefields) around the nucleus are negatively charged. The force-differential between positive/negative charges defines the potential of protons and electrons for atomic-molecular change. Protons and electrons are particulate constituents of all atoms, and while their numbers and dispositions change from element to element, they are the same in all elements. The differential of electrical charge in

51

atoms and molecules gives to electrons their ability to mediate the interactions of atoms and molecules.

Electromagnetism is a phenomenon of charge-differential. As children, many of us played with magnets and discovered the quantum-electric fact that the magnetic positive poles repulse each other, as do negative poles, while the positive and negative poles strongly attract each other. This attraction-repulsion phenomenon of electromagnetism is what makes the generation and usage of electricity practical in so many ways.

The positive/negative charge (proton/electron) makes the harnessing of electricity practical in two common ways, firstly, in the "direct current" flow of electrons (DC) and secondly in the "alternating current" pulsing of electrons (AC). A car battery and flashlight batteries are examples of DC electricity. AC electricity is different. Positive/negative magnetic poles are statically arranged (fixed) in a circle to form a housing, a "stator," and within the cylindrical housing of the magnets a cylindrical core of wound copper wires (the rotor) is inserted and rotated. When a copper wire is rotated within the positive/negative magnetic field, a flow of electrons (pulse) occurs. This is the principle of the electrical generator. Reversing the process, that is, changing in sequence the electrical charge of the magnetic poles in the stator causes the rotor within their fields to rotate. This is the principle of the electrical motor.

The flow of electrons (alternating current) occurs with the induction of magnetic-field-pulsing between the extremes of the maximum positive electrical charge to the maximum negative electrical charge around an electron carrier, e.g., a wire, a nerve net. Midpoint between the wave peaks of the maximum positive and the maximum negative, the charge is neutral. The flow of electrons is in the direction of grounding along the neutral line. Also, electricity flowing through a wire (nerve net) induces an electrical wave field about the wire and along the line of electrical flow. This field around an electrical conductor is called the electromagnetic field (emf), which some believe may pose hazards to health, for example, along high voltage electrical transmission highlines.

The role of micro emfs (in the body) in information-processing (sensation, information storage and recollection) is not to my knowledge a well developed field of study. Collectively, the "vibes" (electron resonance) that define a complex molecular structure are characterized by the complex of joined, interactive electromagnetic fields created by the atomic-molecular complexes. In recent times better understandings of electron interactivity at the atomic-molecular level are advancing communicational technologies, which is virtually putting global peoples in direct contact with each other.

REASON FOR LOVE—CONSCIENCE

Worldly Wisdom vs. Godly Wisdom

Love anticipates. Wisdom-consciousness is a two-pronged consciousness. It addresses both life's ephemeral, immediate needs, as well as life's long term, future needs. Making decisions on bases of the conscious anticipation of the needs for the future as well as for the present is nothing other than the exercise of conscience. Conscience is wisdom's way. The sin consciousness of the Garden-of-Eden story is that of consciousness confused, namely, of the press of immediate appetites (need and greed) and the obfuscation of their mortal consequences in the future. The "First Parents" were held accountable; how much more then are we accountable.

The mortal impacts of need-and-greed appetites are the more consequential when individualistic appetites are institutionally licensed out-of-proportion to need and to the sustainability of natural providence. The disease of institutional myopia (blindness to consequences) is evidenced in the person of St. Peter, the chosen first Church leader whom Jesus called a "satan" because of his political, small-world understanding of the messiah, that is, as an earthly kingdom-builder. Jesus represented in his person, in his example, and in his teaching that his mission was not to worldly kingdom-building but to the well-being (salvation) of all people—to attending to the necessities of the individual and the social future while attending also to the present. "My kingdom is not of this world." The "satanism" of self-aggrandizing kingdom building is an institutional plague threatening future well-being.

One would think that history and the testimony of personal and social experience would enlighten societal consciousness to the fatal threats of excessive, individualistic consumption. In hindsight it is now all too obvious that the mortal consumption of the global garden's "middletree" is dangerously threatening not just to future humankind but also to Earthlife's very global network. The consciousness of global catastrophes, already happened and still happening, should awaken us collectively to make the quantum leap away from the mortal waste of vital sustainability.

In Teilhard de Chardin's word, human consciousness needs to arise to a new "phylum" of cultural insight and recognize that the serpentine cunning of worldly wisdom can be a mortal deceit, a globally catastrophic sin. The worldly wisdom of wasteful consumerism is a Garden-of-Eden self-assertion that clouds human judgment. If God were now to command the Guardian Angel of the Garden to drive humankind from the global Eden for consuming the fruit of the Middletree, would it mean the end to humankind? That answer remains in the future. If human consciousness can make a quantum leap from worldly wisdom to Godly, it may yet again experience that "hope springs eternal." The prevalence of crass consumerism is a mortal myopia in need of correction.

Whither America?

Civilization-wise, where is America today? America's "democracy" is probably best described as "Hegelian feudalism." Hegel eschewed the one-person/one-vote principle of democracy. He believed that citizens (subjectivities) should join a collective, a corporation (objectivity, "estate"), and that the collective should be politically represented rather than the individual. He advocated a strongly authoritarian government, premised in his belief that objectivity resides in the state authority and not in the subjects, for, individually, humans are sin-fated as the fallen offspring of first parents (Augustinian Manichaeism). Hegel extrapolated his religious belief in dualism—the separate adversary realms of spirit and matter—on to the political.

American Democracy is corporation-responsive (where the money is!) more than people-responsive. Elected officials live by and "serve" the exploitive dogma of consumerism. They have allowed the people and resources to be indentured to the will of corporate exploitation, and they promote corporate dominion globally. Thus, institutional Romanism—mythological Romanism—has, in the United States of America, morphed into the aggressive feudalism of corporation-controlled resources. Politically, corporations foment contentiousness, waste and the violations of human rights. But, because the public is as enlightened (potentially) as its leadership, it does not easily countenance willful governmental inauthenticity. Government's underlying philosophy of dualism, adversarily instituted in jurisprudence, infects two-party politics, which also are largely controlled by lawyers. This adversarial political structuring is in question for it lacks people-empowering representation. A functional third-party, representing people interest rather than corporate, could well serve to make the two existing parties more honest before the public.

America, as a civilization, needs to evaluate itself by valuating the morphological relationships (frictional) of the six societal levels of Carroll Quigley ("The Evolution of Civilizations"). Areas needing rethinking and redefinition include:

1) the harm of the spirit/matter schism,
2) the relationship (relativity) of subjectivity/objectivity,
3) corporate vs. people-representation,
4) third-party political advocacy in people-interest,
5) the misdirections of economic/ecologic consumerism, and
6) the hyperculture of violence, in military aggressiveness and in penal codes.

When cultural fixations become civilizational fixtures, the misdirection of morphological frictions become more problematic; their resolution by rational process (communication/consciousness/conscience) is surely the preferred way; but, if the morphological frictions are so entangled, and intolerable, the ultimate resolution may come about only through a mortal festering that creates a boil that bursts on its own. The grief of such a resolution may have radically disruptive consequences. Given contemporary global, civilizational frictions, the prospect of a popped-boil resolution is a horrible thought. Surely it is not too late for rationality to avoid such an unseemly resolution.

OF BLOSSOMS & BUTTERFLIES.
SACRAMENT IS NATURE'S SCRIPTURE. HOW? Matter's designs are sacrament's signs. Sacrament is God's Word/Work ever birthing natural soul/substance. Life's gossamer imprints are Word forms working the seamless fabrics of Word power's designs in resonant nerve nets—the dance of tri-unity.

When Good and Bad Witches Meet

Modern Romanism is a modified social stew first institutionalized in *classical* Rome. The Roman Empire politicized the class divisions of the indentured and those who indenture. Between the slaves and the ruling class was a middle class, which served as a medium between the slavers and the slaves. The political manipulation of public ignorance and fear was used to contain social disquiet. The middle class facilitated the manipulation. But communication and education served to weaken the mechanisms of control. The wizards of control had but a thin stage-curtain separating them from the rebellion of the enslaved.

When slave-work is humanly demeaning it unsettles consciousness. When words are used to defeat open consciousness they foment frustration and a sense of futility. Sense of fulfillment is experienced in self-accomplishment, in a healthy mind/body, word/work balance. A certain amount of drudge is in the life of every person, which should, however, be balanced by a certain amount of leisure and freedom that one owns. Their grossly disproportionate imbalance, as happens when just rewards are missing in life, is violent on its face and cannot long be countenanced by those deprived. Unjust polarities need to be reconciled in order for all to enjoy common humanity.

Dialog is the natural device for reconciling differences. Dialogic resolution is exemplified in paradigmatic nature. Middle-way resolutions are sought from the opposing pull of North/South polarities. East/West "winds" mix up the political options. As stories have it, when the North/South good witches intervene the furies of the East/West bad witches, the amelioration of havoc may happen. The truth is that life's unavoidable, purgatorial witches are provoked by human activities.

In Search of Social Vision

Corporate Myopia: a deeply disabling disease. Experience tells that all suffer the dysfunctions of short sightedness. In his book, "The Evolution of Civilizations," Carroll Quigley selects six social groupings, which in the course of civilizational history have been variously institutionalized and bureaucratized. He uses his six "social levels" to evaluate the historical progress/regress of civilizations; they are: "(1) military, (2) political, (3) economic, (4) social, (5) religious, and (6) intellectual." While membership in his levels overlaps, and people usually belong to several at the same time, each has, nevertheless, evolved an individualistic identity. This is with advantages and disadvantages. [A definition of "civilization" compatible with Quigley's is a communally organized grouping of peoples in a geographical region, which produces life-necessities in sufficient excess as to enable settlement in cities and the use of surplus goods in social commerce.]

Quigley evaluates sequentially the waxing and waning of civilizations by these social factors, mixture, gestation, expansion, conflict, spread, decay and invasion. The institutionalizing and bureaucratizing of his social levels are by internal processes that address group-specialized activities and self-sustainability. Self-interest becomes a self-defining aspect of the group's institutional structure and dynamic (morphology). The instinctual dynamic of self-preservation generates defensive barriers against dilutional influences. Thus, structurally and ideologically, each level self defines its own morphology, which may be benign (promotes civilizational harmony) or malignant (provokes inter-institutional discord). Group morphologies tend to infect their own kinds of civilizational stressors depending on how disharmonious the groups are toward each other. In characterizing evolutionary changes within civilizations, Quigley evaluates the "morphological frictions" amongst groups. In their perceived self-interest, groups structure themselves in ways that interfere with idea-exchanges that dilute ideological self-interest. The idea-exchange that evolves is from within the group, thus tending to make the group introverted in its perspectives and relationships with other groups. Because the fertilization of ideas occurs from within each grouping's family circle, the result is inbreeding that produces an incestuous rationality, which serves more the group interest than the interest of the commonweal.

The in-turned vision of group-rationality frustrates the diversification that normally occurs with the cross-fertilization of ideas from other groups—it is a form of social "monoculturing." Idea inbreeding may in the short-term express genetic vigor, but also weakness. The evolutionary impact of monoclonal ideas is a kind of abhorrence for diversity—a friction-causing kind of "order." Because of their morphologically cultured frictions groups become agents of civilizational disease.

Arguably, Western civilization is now radicalized in institutional myopia, which provokes civil contentiousness. People suffer from being polarized by conflicting institutional "truths," which war for political allegiances. Because of the conflicting voices confusing personal consciousness, people suffer psychological and physical trauma. They suffer radical disconnect from their sustaining connections.

How can this violent period of conflict, now in progress, be cured of its violence? Perhaps before that question can be answered another needs asking: "Are there any overarching social levels, which more than any other engage people in ways that make them potential agents of social harmony?" The answer is yes. There are two overarching levels, the "religious" and the "intellectual," that to some degree engage everyone no matter to what other level(s) (s)he belongs. A major obstacle, however, is that both of these are diseased also by their own incestuous myopia and that they have at the present time perhaps as much morphological friction between and within them as does any other level. Before a common morality (faith) and a common intelligence (reason) can function as leavening agents capable of dissipating morphological frictions in other groups, they must first dissipate their own frictions.

Carroll Quigley, perhaps the 20th Century's premier philosopher of history, has given to the 21st Century a vehicle into historical insight that may open to civilizations a way by which they can self-diagnose and self-correct their self-inflicted diseases. The associations of the *religious* and *intellectual levels* need to confront themselves from history's perspective if they are to overcome their own inauthenticities and become the harmonizing influence that is within their capability.

Faith (religion) and science (intellect) can date approximately the time and circumstances that occasioned their coming to an adversary mind. It was around the times of Copernicus, Galileo Galilei, Giordano Bruno and Rene Descartes (1600). This was a time when the longstanding Earth-centered worldview, espoused in theological reasoning, was assaulted and exposed for its error. This sea change of thinking posed a cataclysmic threat to Earth-man-centered cosmology/philosophy/theology. The tenuous peace that eventually came between science and religion revitalized the old dualisms separating the realms of spirit and matter. The corporate convenience cleaving cosmic continuity for reasons of institutional accommodation has been damaging to human consciousness, whose common venue is inseparably in both realms. Especially in Western civilization, this aggravated schism has given rise to politicized social divisions.

Consistent with Quigley's evaluation method, but dealing very specifically with the schismatic relationship between religion and science, is the book "Eden's Lifework Poetree" by this writer. Along with unearthing frictional relationships corresponding to Quigley's, Steffen's "summa" of societal challenges at the end of the Second Christian Millennium deal especially with the frustrations introduced by institutional church (*religious level*) and science (*intellectual level*) into interpersonal relationships.

When societal structures are politicized on institutional presumptions (e.g., jurisprudence's adversary presumption) that aggravate frictions amongst them, it is inevitable that an agitated state of aggravated conflict will prevail. Before the aggravation can be mitigated, the institutions need to work seriously to eliminate the morphological causes of frictions, and on the positive side, to identify the common grounds on which they can collaborate. Such process is how symbioses work naturally.

There is a long hallowed saying, "vox populi, vox Dei," which loosely translated says, "the people speaks for God." (This was the sense of "church"—The People Church—that came out of the Second Vatican Council of Popes John XXIII and Paul VI.) Of the same genre of thought is the generally accepted maxim that "truth unfolds in the working of communal consciousness." Institutional ideologies that bend truth to self-advantage militate against an authentic, communal consciousness of truth. Histories of civilizations are freighted with distortions of truths by institutions claiming to have God's favor.

The healing of societal frictions cannot happen until they are named, and until there is a will to identify their causes and eliminate them. "Eden's Lifework Poetree" names frictions corresponding with Quigley's six levels, and more, e.g.,

- the wasteful machismo of military assertiveness;
- the homicidal obscenity of global arms peddling;
- the misdirection of the so-called "just war" theory;
- the fraud of economics that trash essential ecology;
- governmental advocacy for the corporate feudalizing of agriculture;
- the corporate bottom-line worship of the greed god;
- law courts exacting the law's letter to kill;
- breaching trust by substituting legality for morality;
- the dishonesty of science with religion, and vice-versa;
- patriarchism's male-instituted idolatry;
- conflicted "truth" that cleaves personal consciousness;
- adversarily polarized politics/government;
- reducing academia to a grist-mill of trivial pursuits; and
- academia and elected servants together pimping for corporate profiteering.

"Eden's Lifework Poetree" doesn't wallow wantonly in finger pointing. It goes beyond mere recitation of societal problems and identifies the process (communication/consciousness/conscience) by which authenticity may flourish and misdirection be corrected. In "poetree" essays and poems personal consciousness is invited to open itself.

- to the natural harmonies of biodiverse landscapes and seascapes;
- to paradigmatic nature, word/worked in essential interdependency;
- to social civility conscionably edified in Earthlife's network of self-awareness;
- to the familial and communal joy experienced in rationally expressed faith, hope, and love;
- to personal well-being, experienced in the consonance of faith and reason; and,
- to universal vitality, which tunes hearts and powers hands.

When a civilization is well ordered it functions like a well-tuned engine. When the engine's sparkplugs' firings are well timed and the mixture of air and fuel is right, the cylinders function in-sync and the engine operates with full power. But when the ignition is out-of-timing the firings of the cylinders defeat the output of power, and the engine balks and smokes and stalls. And that is the way it is in society when people are out-of-tune with each other and with essential continuities. Carroll Quigley's six social levels are like the cylinders of civilization's engine. Their harmonic firing is essential if civilizations would escape being drained of essential power. Out-of-tune engines are notoriously wasteful and polluting. Don't we know!

Biblical writers used a more natural metaphor than a car engine. They used a tree. They recognized the divine mandate to behave reverently and deferentially toward natural providence, toward the tree of vitality "in the middle of the garden"—the "tree of life possessing all knowledge of good and evil." God sternly warned "first parents," under threat of being thrown out of the Garden, not to "consume the fruit" of the middletree. The wreck of the "garden," the waste of Providence happens one choice at a time.

From today's downstream perspective on Earthlife's condition, it is very clear that humankind continues to ignore the scriptural mandate and warning. And because, individually, we assert egoistic self-advantage, we fire our cylinders without concern for being in-sync with other individuals. And so, our civilizations shake, rattle and stall. Natural engines (Earthlife vitality) are (is) being massively frustrated. Global waste is now so out-of-control from the misfiring of societal engines that the greater question isn't how civilizations might thrive but how they can survive the next 1000 years. We should be encouraged, however, that the solution to thriving and surviving is the same— conversion away from an exploitational mindset, from wasteful consumerism to sustainable conservation.

Personal/corporate consumerism is exploitational passion trashing the vitality of the middletree. Nothing in the path of consumerist extravagance is safe. Instituted profiteering is a giant worm wasting the web of life and blasting the fruit of the middletree. Recovery from this deeply disabling disease begins with personal conversion, family conversion, communal conversion, societal conversion from inauthenticity, incivility, to authenticity, civility. Authenticity and civility begin with reverence and deference for cosmic continuity, for the essential vitality of network life—community, for the "middletree fruit," Providence—that must be preserved else we all perish.

UBI CARITAS, IBI DEUS EST.

WHERE ALTRUISM IS, GOD IS.

Word/Work: Agent & Agendum

Theology (*theos*, God; *logos*, word) isn't just word about God, it is about God *as* Word, about the scripture of nature and the nature of scripture still being written and discovered. The ink of scripture is quantum-electric; its hermeneutics (informed interpretation) are dialogically quantum-electric—bigger, and smaller, than life itself. Although largely ignored by traditional Christianity, *quantum-electric substantiation is the quintessential bonding of all existence, of all spirituality*. This quantum-electric fact of soul/substance is an elephant, though largely unseen, in the sanctuary of every church. The malaise infecting Christian Churches is a myopia fixated in staticism, centrism and absolutism.

Cosmic energy/matter is both the agent and the agendum of all change. Inseparably operative, energy/matter ever transforms into the *consciousness* and *construct* of all interdependent soul/substance, spirituality/materiality. Their existential codependency drives evolutionary complexity, transformational necessity. Out of ignorance and arrogance we humans blithely divide what God has joined, and in so doing, we do violence to ourselves and to others. Essential constructs, bonded in forces of quantum-electric attraction, are marriage relationships that edify consciousness as well as physicality. All life's fruitfulness evolves from the codependency (marriage!) of soul/substance. But, the habituated culture of dualistic theologies regularly cleaves soul from body and evolves an abortionist irrationality, a *culture of death*.

That all commonsense rationality is normative to all vitality is self-evident in the evolutionary subtlety of the quantum-electric universe. Electrical consciousness (positive-negative attraction) is the elemental awareness substantiating consciousness in all its gradations of subtlety/complexity. Energetic substantiation, more subtly evolved in complex quantum-electric bonding, is a spiritual/material process of ascendancy—a communally sensitive, rational process of self-consciousness. Violence is done to communal sensitivity when the codependent identity of word/work is violated in/by religion's breach of soul/substance unity.

The energetic substantiation of the quantum-electric universe is the natural (divine) process of cosmic rationality, whose logic is paradigmatic of authentic spirituality in all its simplicity and complexity. Evolution (transformational change) is the unification process of diversified consciousness and substantiation. The energetic subtleties driving all diversified complexities are communicational powers, themselves ever more expansive in their potentials as new subtleties (complexities) are put in place. It must be conceded then that the commonsense of quantum-electric consciousness is the commonsense of human rationality, the naturally conscious soul of intentional, evolutionary symbiosis.

The culturally presumed disconnection of bodily materiality from the soul's spirituality is at the root of disconnected logic, and it drives human inauthenticity in relationships with material realities. The advancing of this misdirected rationality compounds inauthenticity whose manifold by-products of self-destruction are globally manifest. Except and until culturally driven irrationality is exposed and expunged, humankind will continue to prosecute its nonsense rationality.

The rational objective of purposeful judgment is to reason and to act in a manner that best serves individual and common well-being. Communication, consciousness and conscience enable such logical thinking/acting, and deepen faith, hope and love, the witness of purposeful judgment and action. The individual prosecution of process rationality is a subjective enterprise whose collective good serves commonsense.

The consequences of outcomes of scientific endeavor, good and bad, measure and characterize the validity of a specific endeavor. Individual scientific consciousness and the motives behind it qualify at the start the objective validity of a particular scientific endeavor, e.g., motives of profit, beneficiaries, etc. It is naive and dishonest to assume that subjective motivation does not qualify the value-judgments at work in pursuits of science. The same can be said with respect to motives behind theologies, and, indeed, behind all human endeavors. Thus, an informed and commonsensical awareness of the fact of bias and misdirection in every human endeavor should always be present. The "text" guiding common sense rationality is genetically embedded; the circumstances of complex reality are "context," the qualifier of textual rationality.

Authentic human rationality is grounded in the natural logic of symbiosis, the sense of commonsense. The authenticity of every rational enterprise is advanced when prosecuted for the highest purposeful outcomes. The natural role of responsible judgment is to enlighten every action in its purposeful outcomes. Purposeful rationality is with outcomes that inspire new beginnings. When consciousness doesn't foresee outcomes, rationality wayfares and logic fails. Surely, religion and science can together serve the common good when they together function aware of outcomes of purposeful, conscionable works.

"Science" most generally is understood as research study into natural phenomena. In recent times it seems that science, in this sense of the word, has become a religion unto itself in that it sees natural phenomena as time-evolved, self-originating (from the Big Bang), and self-perpetuating without consideration for "being" prior to the Big Bang. But such an attitude is too simplistic, unsatisfactory and short sighted also for the scientific mind, which seeks understandings beyond market utility. There is a broader, more philosophic meaning to the word science, which is, the eclectic cumulus of evident and experienced learning. The perspective of research-science, like that of institutionalized theology, is made too ideological, too qualified in narrow biases and hidden agenda, which radically disallow the openness of *nature's mind.*

The natural process of rationality, of quantum-electric consciousness, is the word/work of intelligibility, religious and scientific, which seeks, in its communal sense, pursuits of life's best explanations, its purposes and needs for achieving life's full symbiotic perfection. Humans act authentically when they seek knowledge less for the purpose to control nature than to obey her.

Cosmic Religion's Rosetta Stone

The physical/psychical universe of natural relationships. More than the orthodoxy of instituted belief, religion is nothing if not a self-aware inner disposition that orders the word/work of personal/communal self-perfecting.

I.   Relativity/Relationship/Religion: the dynamic soul of transformational matter.

Cosmology deals with the Science of the universe. (Physica).
    NOVOGENESIS—Process Cosmology/Physica.
Metaphysics deals with the Philosophy of consciousness. (Metaphysica).
    METAGENESIS—Process Philosophy/Metaphysica.
Theology deals with the Morality of conscionable relationships. (Ethica).
    THEOGENESIS—Process Theology/Ethica.

II. Worldviews:

1.) The Centrist: it is premised in Aristotle's (Thomas Aquinas') Earth-centered, stable-state (static) universe, that is, in "Physica," Aristotle's natural order of being, and "Metaphysica," being-as-being, his rationale of divine attributes. **2.) The Transformational**: it is premised in the energetic, quantum-electric substantiation (atomic structuring) of matter (MC^2) always-in-process, and in accord with the Continuity of Purpose.   Moment-by-moment contingencies are with consequence to outcomes. *Personal choices do matter.*

Are these two worldviews reconcilable? Cosmologically? Philosophically? Theologically? Which is acceptable to modern public consciousness? Which is acceptable to your consciousness? Is a theology, premised on static-centrist presumptions, credible today in the face of general public experience and knowledge? Is traditional, Christian theology suffering a loss of public credibility because of its absolutist, static-centrist presumptions? What is the object of life's striving? Making way for Christ in "second comings'?

Sylvester L. Steffen

The Sacrament of God Present

The way. The truth. The light.
Communication/consciousness/conscience.
Faith. Hope. Love.
Resurrection. Ascendance. Transcendence.

WORD is the Nurtural Expression of God's Presence (Soul)
WORK is the Natural Expression of God's Presence (Body)
In WORD/WORK, Nurture/Nature expresses God's Presence.

<u>SIGN</u>   <u>GRACE</u>

I. The SACRAMENTS OF NATURE. (Body : Substance).

  Water.   **Baptism**—original life's edification.   Faith.

  Sun/Air. **Eucharist**—soul/body transformation.   Hope.

  Soil.   **Anointing**—sacrificing self for others.   Love.

II. The SACRAMENTS OF NURTURE. (Spirit : Soul).

  Wisdom. **Confession**—assenting to God's Truth. Faith.

  Age.   **Confirmation**—embracing God's Truth. Hope.

  Grace. **Priesthood**—serving God's Truth.   Love.

III. The VOCATIONAL SACRAMENTS. (Nurture / Nature).

  Partnership. **Marriage**—male/female covenant. Family Harmony.

  Community. **Holy Orders**—public covenant. Societal Harmony.

IV. The AFFECTS and EFFECTS of SACRAMENTS are

  Ex opere operato—unreflective intensionality—quantum-electric.

  Ex opere operantis—reflective intentionality—physical/rational.

Unless the Seed Dies

SUBSTANCE-IDENTIFIED SOUL.
When Isaiah says that *all flesh is grass*
He means to say that all self-conscious vitality
Is a development of photosynthesis. And so it is.

The theology of self-negation: life ends, life continues. This apparently contradictory awareness is a great mystery. It is an age-old theme of spirituality that finds great inspiration in the near desperation of Jesus in the Garden of Olives when he prayed, "Father, if it is possible let this cup pass from me." A little later he recovered his composure and resolutely accepted the inevitable, "Let thy will be done, not mine." With these words Jesus entered upon the final, willful "pouring out" of himself (in the word of St. Paul "exinanivit").

I recall an embarrassing moment in philosophy class when I came one morning not well prepared. Of course, the first question asked by the professor (Father Vincent Fecher, S.V.D.) was directed to me. I recall sputtering out in Latin some incoherent words that were hardly to the point. My final point was, "mysterium est." At this the class couldn't contain itself for my obvious chagrin, and it lost it with this last profound pronouncement. Father Fecher allowed himself a wry smile and commented, almost too quietly to be heard, *Pro tibi, fortasse, non aliis."* (Maybe for you, but not for the others.) Since then I find no mystery too unapproachable that I shouldn't try to increase my understanding of it.

The phrase, "unless the seed dies," has *quantum-electric* meaning. The DNA coding in the seed's germ activates seedling growth in response to external factors, and over time brings the seedling to maturity. In early growth the seedling assimilates the degrading food stores of the parent seed. In the eventual production of new seeds, the plant "pours itself out" and disintegrates. But, its life continues on in the dormant new seeds produced by the mature plant.

From the seed's food stores the embryo assembles very early the chlorophyll molecules, which function as the construction material suppliers. Chlorophyll, the green-cell mechanism of plants, *mysteriously* enables plants to capture light (photons) and carbon dioxide, and to restructure the water and carbon dioxide molecules into the glycogen (CHOH, carbohydrate) agency, which is the plant's self-edifying architecture. The triatomic tensions of molecular water and carbon dioxide are tuned to attenuate the harmonic energy of infrared waves in the electromagnetic spectrum. Powered by photons, the process of photosynthesis disassembles water and carbon dioxide and reassembles them into carbohydrates in ratios of one carbon atom to one water molecule. For every carbon atom used, one oxygen molecule (O_2) is released into the atmosphere. [As Tompkins and

Bird write in the introduction to their book *The Secret Life of Plants* (Avon Books, 1974, p. ix): "Without green plants we would neither breathe nor eat. On the undersurface of every leaf a million moveable lips are engaged in devouring carbon dioxide and expelling oxygen".] (Also, see Book Ten of *Eden's Lifework Poetree*.) After the plant's death, its vitality continues on in the seeds that it produces.

For us, this consciousness takes new turns when we meditate on Isaiah's words, "All flesh is grass." (Is 40 4). We are forced to anticipate the eventual coming of our bodies to be *dead straw*. The word "exinanivit" especially applies to mothers who pour themselves out in bringing to full life the conceptus in their wombs. Spiritually and practically, there is a profound lesson for all of us, even though we do not experience this mystery in the same way that a mother does.

The gradual disintegration of our bodies is part of aging, culminating ultimately in the failure of vital continuity—death—and the atomic/molecular surrender of vitality (energy). If we fail to reconcile ourselves to this dissolution reality, for whatever reasons, the thought of death can depress us. The process of self-reconciliation is sometimes very difficult for it is a part of the evolved consciousness sometimes referred to as the "dark night of the soul." Nevertheless, faith tells us that death is gain, not loss.

In the recent past, the politicized vogue of ego-centrism, among other reasons, led to a philosophical strand of thought called "nihilism," a fatalistic and despairing attitude toward life's worth. When personal self is the life-focus, selfishness arises, and because personal life must end with death, selfishness knows it has no future. Desperation follows. Optimism, purpose and hope have everything to do with relationships with others—all those relationships that sustain us—and these are "communal." We are self-fulfilled only by living in harmonic relationship with all that sustains us. This much we know, upon death we live on in communal relationship. How else we may live on after death isn't knowable to us, no matter what speculations we dream up. Faith lets loose.

The lessons of our personal living live on in the lives of those with whom we have communed. When we realize, *really realize*, "Christogenesis"— that every newborn is a Christ of Second Coming—we can then grow into an appreciation of how fortunate we are to be able "to prepare the way of the Lord" by pouring ourselves out as a gift for those who come after us. In this realization, self-negation—consciousness of the inevitability of self-diminution, of the expenditure of self—is illuminated as an essential process of real purpose.

Heaven. Purgatory. Hell.

Life is the expanding venture of self-aware consciousness, radiating omni-directionally in harmonic diversifications. Life is, both journey and quest, a journey of ever opening horizons, and a quest that searches particulate chaos for serendipitous diversifications. The journey-quest builds on relationships—relationships of possibilities harmonized in the compatible frequencies of particulate liaisons. Compatibilities, harmonically established in matter (mass, structure), are the substantive bases, the "subsidiarities" that essentially underlie all subsequent relationships.

Creativity is word-woven in creation, in cosmic continuity; it is self-expanding in soul/substance, itself more than the soul/substance of continuity's definition in time/space, and, infinitely unqualifiable in terms of the ultimate definities of expanding continuities. The Creator is Word-involved in Creation. We are process-defined in Word-destiny. We are spiritually substanced qualifications of infinite subsidiarities whose consciousness actively participates in the divinely creative Presence. My hands are God's hands. My thoughts are God's thoughts. My voice is God's. Eternally.

In its self-assumed God-standing over people, Church hierarchy imposes on itself the unattainable demand of behaving Godlike, when in fact it behaves as humanly as everybody else. Superhuman self-arrogation is a heavy and gratuitous imposition. Hierarchy is destined to disappoint public expectations. Purgatory is the tortuous trial of relationships seeking harmony and overcoming disharmony—the perpetual struggle of self-coming to symbiotic accommodation. Symbiotically accommodated communities are expressions of God's communion in energy/matter/time/space—in the here-and-now. The struggle of coming to symbiotic accommodations is the great jihad, the purgatory of God's life-perfecting work—the transformational way to perfected relationship, to "heaven." Hell is the willful doing of things that one knows does violence to God's scripted laws in nature—it is the intentional flaunting of dissonance—in God's face—the knowing sacrilege of natural symbioses.

Civil Violence

Patriarchism, theocracy, and nationalism are discriminatory and violent models. For purposes of joining problematic issues, a premise will be stated and connections given, which may or may not be true. The point of this exercise is to circumscribe a ring in which contemporary, hot-button issues can be joined.

Statement: cultural male self-electionism (patriarchy) is a deeply rooted agency causing interpersonal violence and ecologic/economic waste.

Connection 1: *elitist male-electionism*, long cultured, brings likeminded males into self-expressive associations that have anti-social consequences, a.) undisciplined possessiveness and control over Earth resources, other life, including other humans presumed inferior, b.) interpersonal sexual exhibits including biases against women, and c.) the societal institutionalization of religious/national (Judeo-Christian) male-electionism.

Connection 2: *breaches and alienation*, a.) alliances affirming male-on-male preferences, b.) obsessing over "ownership" of females who in self-defense move into female-on-female relationships, and c.) the calculated rejection of males by females for male unfitness and scandal as parental models.

Conclusion: Women (and men!) must reject and confront idolatrous patriarchism in all its unjust facets in order to reverse globally the downhill slide toward ultimate havoc now being visited on societies by acculturated *religious* patriarchism.

ESSENTIAL GENESIS
Human enterprise,
also religion, is grist
of the cosmic mill.

NATURE & NURTURE

Do children "become" their parents? While the fact of Big Bang singularity may explain nature's unity of plurality, and, chaotic diversification may explain nurture's plurality from unity, the mystery of first origins is not resolved. The infinity of the source-regression of energy/matter, of soul/substance, projects back into a past too vast to be grasped, notwithstanding the human penchant to speculate back beyond its competence.

Humankind is a global community of subjects (subjectivities). From the faith perspective, solidified experientially in reason, it is commonly believed that all subjectivity (singularity) and all community (plurality) are possessed in God. Thus, individual/communal likeness to God derives from intentional harmony. Communal virtue, the collectively attenuated energy of faith, hope and love, is a subtle complexity of evolved consciousness. These virtues are attributes of the Godhead Persons reflectively refined in human relationships. In that the human conception of the Godhead is shaped by human rationality it cannot escape transformation as human consciousness changes.

Certitude and truth are reinforced in the conscious dialog of family-community, wherein well-being is secured in the mutually serving relationships of family-community members. The coming together of science/religion (reason/faith) occurs in the informed mutuality of interdependents, which secures the common vitality of network interdependency that has sustained, presently sustains, and sustains into the future all vitality. The symbiotic lesson revealed in diversified life is the quintessential necessity of willful, individual endeavor motivated in common well-being.

Communal well-being is secured in the diverse expressions of creative individuality that serves the individual/social good. Service that builds community sustains; what does not build community disserves. The transforming role of individuality is self-fulfilling when it is motivated in communal well-being. The motivation of human consciousness, individual and institutional, must be in communal service if self-fulfillment is to be accessible to all.

All subjectivity is grist in the mill of quantum-electric change. No less than humans themselves, institutions must change. The rational energy driving individual/institutional change is holistic philosophy, a consciousness born from the communication of individuals (subjectivities) in the grinder of societal frictions. For the individual, lifelong communication begins in the family. And, on the bases of parental continuity, a child is, in the characterization of his/her nature/nurture an extension of his/her parents. For the individual's lifetime, father/mother consciousness within speaks to the individual's consciousness. Mind and body, we are our parents.

The two-step (inductive/deductive) reasoning process of experience is everybody's way of advancing in consciousness—of doing philosophy—whether or not it is recognized in those terms. Upon the inductive/deductive legs of rationality, faith and certitude, religion and sanity (well-being) advance. Rational science, informed thinking, individually and collectively, as daily employed in practical living, and collectively, as a body of thought (philosophy), needs the continual corrective of inductive/deductive dialogue.

Even though practiced rationality, like breathing, reflexly/reflectively interweaves inductive information with deductive analyses, analytic compartmentalizing has distinguished the two processing modes from each other in a way that divides the function of their unitary processing. "Science," inductive inquiry, as a methodology of research seems to function as a process unto itself free of accountability to deductive analyses, which accommodate data in terms of impacts on holistic well-being. All realms of learning have in the past belonged to the field of Philosophy. It's only within the last several centuries that Philosophy has lost its inclusionary, integrative role of processing new learning into a holistic consciousness advanced from generation to generation.

Since the times of Giordano Bruno, Galileo Galilei and René Descartes (after 1600) the philosophy of deductive learning (information, value-processing) has been given over to institutional religion while inductive learning (scientific research) has been given over to institutional science. The turf of Philosophy has been divided and appropriated by the competing realms of "spirituality" and "materiality." The first victim of this turf battle is Philosophy itself, and ultimately, humans and network life. The psychical disease of global schizophrenia (uprooting the psychical from the physical) and the physical trashing of Earthlife are inheritances of cleaved spirituality/materiality. Since this theft of the knowledge-turf by religion and science, inductive and deductive syntheses of learning have grown apart, as have religion and science, as well as their credibility and service to the public. Public harm from this schism will continue to expand so long as the unification of learning is held hostage by the adversary ideologies of institutional religion and science.

The "friend of wisdom" (philosopher) is one who engages the mutually informing processes of inductive/deductive learning. Philosophically, such a person is a "generalist" for (s)he relates new and particular learning to the vast body of knowledge; whereas, the person who narrows his/her field of study to a particular field of study is a "particularist" ("science" in its usual meaning). It is fair to say that a philosopher is a generalist while research scientists and theologians are particularists; their vision is captured in narrow fields of study. The disease risk associated with the particularist is "myopia" for (s)he may tend to give exaggerated value to her/his narrow expertise, which may lack a broader knowledge-base against which to weigh relative values. The remedy to partiality toward values is to see all in the context of the *unity of knowledge*, not just in the individual profession, but in the cumulus of holistic learning. Truth itself is validated in the proportional relationships of applied inductive/deductive learning, as are certitude and credibility.

No matter where we are in our lives, the question as to how the prevailing worldview influences our upbringing is a question that matters. We may phrase the question in this way, "Do children become their parents?" It is a question of 1) theology, 2) history, 3) psychology, 4) biology, and 5) physics. Answers to this multifaceted question are found in the correlated understandings of inductive/deductive science, and they bear directly on the authenticity of interpersonal relationships. The question also bears directly on the all-important matter as to whether or not the human family will advance on the way of spreading more havoc and destruction or self-redemption and social harmony.

Theological question. Christianity advances the belief that while the substance of the human body may be a product of evolution, not so the soul which is individually created by God and given residence in an individual body. The evolution of consciousness seems to be factually evident; its complexity is characteristic of substance (neural) complexity. Is "soul" different from consciousness? Does soul individually have existence outside of substance complexity? In what way is it transcendent? Consciousness, as inter-relational awareness and interactivity, is an inherited complexity inhering in evolved, substantive complexity. Evolved substance is inseparable from the awareness complexity that energizes it and gives it coherency. In a lifetime, vital complexity, i.e., conscious substance, spirituality/materiality, changes. The "energy aura" (*noosphere*) inhering and enveloping individual personality evidences the *electric* vitality (soul) of individuality and is a phenomenon of molecular harmonics. Personality evolves individually in soul/substance, and, humans do not experience individuality (subjectivity) except in joined soul/substance. Self-conscious experience knows that the *human soul is conscious* and that self-aware consciousness endures dependently on/in vitally embodied substance.

Inherent vitality, as codified in DNA, self-transmits from generation to generation. And, as genetic coding is responsive to (transformed by) experiential contingencies, so is soul/substance. God is operative in phylogeny as well as in ontogeny. God's involvement is not lessened by the fact that ontogeny in all its facets is a product of phylogeny. Individually received genetics qualify individuality, spirituality. "Received genetics" are material (natural) as well as spiritual (nurtural), that is, they are received in the experiential relationships that occur in the lifetimes of parents and children. So, by reason of received genetics, children do "become" their parents, for better or for worse. This does not mean to say that children are fated to be as their parents. Time and time again, children who have been raised in desperate family circumstances turn out to be exemplary in virtuous living; it works the other way, too, children who have lived in apparently idyllic family circumstances sometimes become global terrorists. Nevertheless, in soul and body, children possess in many ways the personalities of their parentage.

It is a fact of experience that children carry personality characteristics of their parents. Thus, parents and society cannot take lightly their collaborative obligation to nurture children, soul and body. As is well known, the real lessons of life are experientially acquired, which means that children learn to do or not to do by what their parents and society do and don't do. Trust is breached when example isn't consistent with words. Parents and society, motivated by egoism and greed, will produce egoistic and greedy children, no matter the admonitions they give to children. Conversely, if parents and society exemplify altruism, children will more likely acquire the virtue of altruism. This nexus, "like parents/like children," applies to the whole gamut of virtues and vices.

Theologically, to live virtuously is to live God-like, and Godlikeness is a received personality of nature/nurture. It is an individually possessed sense of communal connection, a harmonized consciousness of diversified unity. The harmonizing of individuality in community is Godlikeness. Life in all its complexity and interdependency is a gift of God. The better we understand this, the better we may understand God and virtuous life. So, it seems socially critical that we realize that our children become us and that we need to be prepared to assume the role of responsible parenting before we become parents.

Historical question. The answer to the historical question is found in the evidence of history. History is the "fact" record in time of individual and social relationships brought forward. The conflicts between good and evil behavior brought forward in societies is the macrocosm of the interpersonal conflicts of good and evil. Ignorance, that is, not knowing any better, causally instigates conflicted relationships; arrogance, the inconsiderate assertion of personal opinion over the opinions of others, causes conflicts; and greed, an obsessive appetite for acquiring things far in excess of personal need also causes personal and social conflicts. Just as love is a logical consequence of altruism (other-concern), so hate is the "logical" rationality of practiced ignorance, arrogance and self-preferring greed. Love arises out of the culture of virtue while animus arises out of the culture of vice (disregard for others). The conflicts of virtue and vice, of love and hate, are the stuff of human history and willful destructiveness.

The cultivation of knowledge and well-being (communication), and the affirmation of awareness (consciousness) that derives from knowledge as it affects relationships, constitutes the human story. The transmission of historical knowledge, the retelling of the story of human evolution, is a work of science (Philosophy, deductive learning) no less than research, investigating particularity, (inductive learning) is a science. The signs of the times seem to evidence that humans fail miserably the rationality of historical insight. Because human rationality is lopsidedly egoistical and selfishly motivated, ignorance, arrogance and greed make up the vicious trinity warring too successfully against the virtuous trinity of faith, hope and love. The deception of anti-social individuality must be recognized for the destructive force that it is. As long as we live anti-socially (consumptively) and transmit to our children this socially destructive example, it will continue to rampage Earthlife like a roaring lion and consume all in its way.

Mind (science, fact knowledge-experience) and heart (myth-story-religion) need to be mutually informing. We may think of myth-religion-story as the deductive leg of informed consciousness, and science-experience-fact-knowledge as the inductive leg. The quest of certitude is a quest of intelligence, the quest of truth. Intellectual inquiry is a quest of science. The collective consciousness of public intelligence (the prevailing worldview) reflects the vogue of religion/science. Religion and science impact contemporaneously on each other. When they conflict in individual consciousness they create societal conflicts. Myths of the times, stories conveying religious/scientific consciousness of the times, are the "generalist" expression of the public consciousness of the times. It expresses the contemporary mix of information and misinformation. It is the role of the continuing process of acquiring new and particularized knowledge to correct misinformation. If the religious/scientific story doesn't change and conform to newly obtained information it betrays the trust of generations to come. Such betrayal is certain to be exposed in due time, and with its exposure, the collapse of institutions built on misinformation.

Psychological question. If the answer is "yes" to the psychological question "Does the soul of parents become the soul of their child?", what is the message to parents? To society? Very simply, that they, we, are obliged by the rationality of commonsense to be honest with truth and to live and voice honesty. To live honestly, truthfully, is to live relationally in a manner that affirms personal and social well-being. This means relating to all other in a subject-to-subject consciousness that sustains the mutuality of otherness and avoids the havoc of ignorance, arrogance and greed.

Biological question. Genetics, history and psychology tell us that, "we are our parents." So, what kind of parents do we want to be to our children? We should want to model the kind of parenting that we want our children to model to their children. We live for the future by living responsibly in the present. In our relationships with all other codependent existence we should model reverence, respect and a sense of subjective equality even if our subsistence requires the consumption of life. Consumption should never be so total as to destroy the codependent network that gives us our shelter and sustenance. Commonsense requires this minimum rationality. We should afford for others no less than for ourselves access to the necessities that enable well-being and self-fulfillment. By the authentic engagement of communication, consciousness and conscience we exemplify the virtues of faith, hope and love, and enable sustainable well-being.

Physical question. We have come full circle now and we return to the original thesis, which posits the quantum-electric (dialogic) nature of all cosmic reality and the transformational necessity of soul/substance. The future, toward which we tend, is one in which perceived outcomes, whether, physical, biological, psychological, historical or religious, are all new beginnings. Outcomes and beginnings are the essential continuities of the cosmos. The conscious continuity of cosmic transformations, the fact basis of human experience, is the deep reason for the obvious necessity of changing from a static-centrist-absolutist worldview to an acentric, transformational one. Belief and certitude find their credibility in the process of rationality, which itself roots in the transformational necessity of essential continuity. This conclusion is the essential lesson of Primary Scripture. Scriptural wisdom endorses the consciousness that we be "clever as snakes but harmless as doves."

Interpersonal Eucharist

FAITH.	HOPE.	LOVE.
COMMUNICATION.	COMMUNION.	COMMUNITY.
TRUST.	ALTRUISM.	SERVICE.

GOD IS WHERE EUCHARIST IS,
IN THE TRIMORPHIC RESONANCE OF COMMUNICATION/
CONSCIOUSNESS/CONSCIENCE.
IN FAITH/HOPE/LOVE, WE EXPERIENCE, PERSONALLY AND
SOCIALLY, THE ECSTASY OF
RESURRECTION, ASCENDENCE AND TRANSCENDENCE.

Trust

It is my conscious effort to plumb the Center of all consciousness for the good purpose of finding the central place of Self in the middle estate of soul/substance. Consciousness' processing of resurrection, ascendance, and transcendence, that happens in the harmony of communication, consciousness and conscience, is a centering work that attenuates the energy of Allness. At the heart of all centering is *The Ineffable,* wherein allness is profoundly subtle and expression fails except by harmonic attenuation—openness' language, which originates and sustains allness. Openness to chaos is there present. At the central void chaos sparks the infinitesimal percentage of order, which bothers about our relationships. Except for chaos there could be no serendipity, no vital diversity. Divine experience produces diverse culture. The promotion of diversification is the Eucharistic blessing of Providence. The Tower of Babel Story tells of the action that God took because he feared for good reason the prospect of monocultural outcomes that would result from a single language, from a centrist *religious* insight. Liberation Theology's "Base Communities" are God's voice again in our time speaking to the arrogance of monolithic church, "I will confuse its tongue lest in coming to one voice it does whatever it has a mind to do."

Consciousness is an inundating tide that emanates from the undulations of original gravity waves. Consciousness is the subtle refinement of energetic production, which finds its first liberty in the Big Bang release of gravity waves. The leaf fluttering on a tree, the waving branch, and the wind that drives the fallen leaves are subtleties of gravity wave continuity. Humans are a genre of leaves, responsive to gravity wave subtleties. All of the cosmos is qualified in gravity wave relationships, subtly articulated at the quantum-electric level.

Story and poetry are about consciousness, the common well of purposeful vitality, of the commonweal. In metaphor and in fact, water is the medium of consciousness. Water is consciousness, the interpenetrating fluid connection in all vitality and of all transformation. The written line of a poem is a wave of thought, which adds its distinctiveness to life's tide flow. The coming together of symmetered lines constitutes the poem's tide, forming, coming to crest, and pounding home its message. Poetry is a tide continuum composed of lines of word and wave that crest individually and compositionally. The lines, the waves constituting the tide are centered, natural compositions deserving middle-estate positioning on the page. So, I hope, deserves the gravity of my poetry.

Female and male together give substance to the poetry of the soul. Equivalently and specifically, female and male characterize human nature in the dance attenuation of consciousness. Ritual dance manifests their synchronicity. Relationships informed in faith, hope, and love attenuate graces of divine presence. Males represent the Godhead no more and no less than females. Thus, in the ministry of Godhead graces, man is no more called and no less called than woman. In that religious priesthood pertains to the ministry of Godhead graces in the context of natural/divine relationships, woman is equally called to priesthood as man. God's salvific grace is sacrileged when the priestly role of woman is countermanded by male arrogance. All society now suffers severely from the sacrilege of priesthood perpetrated on global life by arrogant patriarchism. The many catastrophes now visiting upon us collectively demand that we desist from our sacrilege and that we repair the havoc wreaked by our ignorance, arrogance and unbridled greed. In the electionism and dead centrism of monocultural patriarchy, the essential spirituality of quantum-electric sexuality is frustrated.

Already in the early years of our formation, the all-important question presents itself, "What shall be my lifework?" If we want a life-fulfilling answer to this quest we probably best seek for it in paradigmatic nature, the Primary Scripture. Contained in the question is the query "how, in the context of my bio-spirituality, can I achieve my highest level of personal fulfillment?" The "holy grail" of life-fulfillment, while universally compelling, must be developed in the reality of personal uniqueness, that is, in the context of my regional, bio-social personality. "Bio-social" includes the bioregional (ecological network) context of my uniqueness, and the sociological (social web) context of my culture. The "text" of my person is biological, genetic, while the "context" of my person is familial, communal. Biologically, my person is a natural continuum; sociologically, it is a nurtural continuum. We are born into the natural/nurtural tide-stream, and all the good and bad that it carries. Our lives begin in, and we begin to work out our lifework in the bio-social contexts of our individual persons; but through communication and acquired consciousness we are not forced to restrict our lifetime work within the narrowly defined text/context of our origins. Motivations of altruism (love) that come from our personal exercises of communication and consciousness can put our life-fulfillment in global contexts as well as local.

Altruism

The energy of youth pushes us to venture beyond the surroundings of our birth and into the open realms of natural diversification that are open to us. But always, we cannot escape the fact of our existence that our personal unfolding is seamlessly bound to the continuity of network life that is our personal origin, sustenance and terminus. We make our way within the milieu of natural continuity by way of communication, consciousness and conscience, if we would be true to ourselves, to our predecessors and our successors. When we are true to these, we behave "authentically." This trimorphic process is the authentic rational process that opens to us a lifetime of "grail" self-fulfillment. At each step on the way of our life process there is hidden "grail" in the bush waiting to be found, which informs us as to open choices in the next step we take. Grail wisdom is a drink of contextual consciousness, which enables us to experience relationships with others, which are fulfilling for them as well as for ourselves. Love for others, altruistic choosing, is the grail work that strengthens us in resolves that are mutually self-fulfilling. In our resolve to sustain all other, to live lightly on Earth, we augment for life our personal experience of faith, hope and love, and, by the ripples of our living, we, together with others, swell materially the resource tide for the commonweal, and spiritually the conscious tide of resurrection, ascendance and transcendence. In so doing we come to the experience of "ecstatic resonance."

We the People are globally awash in misdirection. The tangled mess of historical inauthenticity, the interactive complexity of generations motivated in ignorance, arrogance and greed, cries for resolution, for it now blinds us in our authentic grail-quest. Inauthenticity's tangled webs can only be untangled by reversing processes that produce it. Day-by-day, minute-by-minute choices of authenticity may let us unwind the mess and repair the damage. If we attempt to confront the mountainous ball in its totality we are likely to be frustrated. But if we deal with inauthenticity in bits and pieces as we are confronted by it in our daily, hourly, bioregional context, the untangling of it becomes more manageable. We cannot undo the past but we can make repairs in the present. We are not without a precedence by which we can be enlightened in our work. We carry in every cell of our body the proven text of Primary Scripture—evolutionary symbiosis—paradigmatic nature, which informs us experientially if we but tune our consciousness to its lessons. Nature opens choices to us when we open our consciousness to the self-destruction caused by the exploitation and waste of natural diversity. Life is genetically programmed to increase diversifications and options. Corporate marketing eschews natural diversity for it frustrates the control corporations must have in order to profiteer from natural "commodities." In the logic of corporate marketing, people need to be made dependent on the goods and services of the corporation, and be denied ad hoc access to natural resources of food and fiber. The bioregional exchange of goods and services is done in a more sustainable manner; people of conscience need to be sensitive to natural networks and not let themselves be treated as wheels of waste that run the machines of corporate profiteering. Multinational conglomerates treat people and resources of Earth as expendable commodities. Collectively we need to develop patterns of resourcing which avoid the control structures of giant corporations. Bioregional sustainability is advantaged by seeking and providing goods and services within one's own region; in so doing capital resources are not drained and use benefits include the revitalization of resources natural to the region. Export production should be measured for it tends to drain regional resources; imports may help mitigate the drain if the associated disposables are recyclable.

How can we shut down the fast road of ecological waste, environmental pollution and social degradation? By recognizing within our own bioregion the inauthenticities of personal behavior that contribute to these. We cannot make a difference by living in isolation. We can make a difference by working together and conforming our cultural practices to constraints imposed by naturally sensitive ecologies and life systems. Diversified food and fiber production systems need to be engaged rather than those of persistent monoculturing. Animal and plant production need to serve each other so that by rotation of crops and usage of animal waste the land is beneficially fertilized and not polluted or depleted. The bioregion can continue to sustain us only if we secure its naturally evolved vitality.

Genetically Modified Organisms (GMOs) present at least two serious biological problems. The first being that genetic modification reduces diversely distributed characteristics into a single production strain, thus, genetic modification is calculated to reduce biological diversification by crowding out other plant and animal species. Secondly, the sequencing of CTGA on the double helix has everything to do with biological expression, which is genetically *texted* across the long historical context of trial-and-error. Gene-splicing intervenes sequencing in ways with unknown consequences. Toxicities introduced into pollen dust is a potential threat. Seriously harmful consequences may not surface except over a long period of time, after which it may be too late to reverse their catastrophes. A somewhat analogous situation now occurring is the excessive use of antibiotics, which has triggered the response in organisms of evolving ways to beat it. Antibiotics have occasioned the evolution of more virulent organisms.

Continuing educational strategies, community and person-to-person meetings about ways of utilizing and preserving bioregional resources, can heighten public consciousness and prepare our children in matters of connections, which may ameliorate or compound environmental and ecological stressors already at work.

When we understand, in the specific, cause-and-effect relationships we are enabled to make better choices.

Service

Kitchen table theology. Theology, the conscious cultivation of relationship with God in the service of others, happens one-on-one, in small group relationships. The conscionable pursuit of authentic, interpersonal relationships is the "doing of theology," for it seeks living harmoniously in relationship with the "Being in whom is all relationship." In this definition, God is perhaps best understood and best worshipped. This definition brings God directly into every action which is motivated in the determination to be "authentic," that is, being concerned for all other as one is for oneself. In living out this determination the mandate to "love God and your neighbor as yourself" is fulfilled and our grail-quest is realized.

Church happens at the kitchen table when people join and together seek to discern how they can best live in a life-sustaining manner. When we open ourselves up to the fact of our personal inauthenticities, we dispose ourselves to be enlightened by the insights of others who can help us come to authenticity. However, given the webs of inauthenticity that entangle us we find it difficult to sort out the authentic from the inauthentic. The long engrained culture of ego-centric thinking and living makes it difficult to discover paradigmatic nature's authentic word and work. This fact speaks to the need of experienced and informed people who can recognize the difference between what is authentic and what is not. The venue of this discernment is found in the "material" order of things (work), which is energized in the "spiritual" (word).

What is specifically proposed here is that the "religious" meets the "secular" on equivalent terms, and that communities of religious men and women serve the public by preparing people who can go out and sit with the public at the kitchen table, in the specific bioregional circumstance, and join dialogue across the whole communal spectrum in order to identify inauthenticities that are eroding the sustainable prospects of communal well-being. Religion, Church, succeeds when the good word/work of Eucharist happens everyday at every kitchen table. *People are Church* when God-consciousness inspires all personal relationships. Relationship is not individualistic, nor is religion—"Where two or three gather there am I with them."

Under the insightful guidance of informed leadership people can re-evaluate locally activities that are rightly ordered and those that are not. But, if the "spiritual" is cleaved from the "material," as church has tended to do, the effort will be futile. Perhaps a common premise for value-discernment is the recognition that each of us brings to the table a level of ignorance, arrogance and greed—for so we are culturally conditioned—and that through communication, consciousness and conscience these can be remediated for personal and communal well-being.

Reward

We come to life's reward in the consciousness of "sacred purpose," *sacra ment*. We are to each other "subject," with whom all other must subjectively relate, that is, they must tolerate our individuality and we must tolerate theirs. What is "absolute" is the sum total of all subjectivity—the transformational necessity that we are personally compelled to accommodate. The infinity of reality, although it is contingently subjective, is the "absolute" within which contingent subjectivity is born, sustained and reclaimed. In our consciousness of the transformational "absolute" experience tells us that we are temporarily necessary agents destined to qualify the transformational continuum, for good or for bad, or for a little of both. All subjectivity is impermanent in structure but not necessarily in effect. We cannot reverse the fact that someday we will no longer be, physically, but we can qualify our presence now in a manner that insures that its effects will be consequential on into the future. When our present subjectivity-complex loses its energetic coherency (vitality) we die—the coherency of our quantum-electric substance dissolves. And after that, what for us? It isn't for us to know, except that love remains.

But what after-life reward can we anticipate? The experience of faith tells us that love endures. It is faith's understanding that God is love. The love we have cultivated in our lives lives on after us in ways that we cannot know in the specific. If for our lifetime we have conscientiously attended to common well-being, it is a certainty then that the love of our living will be amplified in the lives of those who are touched by the love we've lived.

St. John the Baptist perhaps epitomizes best the committed consciousness that we wisely should entertain throughout our lives. Scripture tells that in his mother's womb John was aware of Jesus' presence even in Mary's womb. John's keen sense of mission and privilege was to prepare the way for one "whose sandal he was unworthy to loose." If we truly believe that every newborn is a Christ of Second Coming, then we know in truth that others who will come after us deserve our heart-full commitment in preparation for their coming. To the extent that we do, the mission of God in others will be more fully perfected.

The faith-compulsion of this understanding surely satisfies our reasonable expectations for reward. We do well to pray daily for the faith-conviction of this understanding, for, by so doing we dispose ourselves to a harmonious relationship with God and we reciprocally return to God the same unconditional love that's been given to us.

Family

Perhaps more important than ferreting out the negative is affirming the positive, for example, collaborating with neighbors to develop agriculture (community) in sustainable directions, directions that increase biodiversity rather than diminish it. The trite saying has it, "when the going gets tough, the tough get going." It is tough in agriculture now, all the more reason for not giving up easily. As family and community we are all in this together. After all, the land is the parent and sustainer of all human life, farmers' as well as townspeople's. The more we learn about ourselves, the more we discover the lesson of Primary Scripture, that we are earth, that Earth is us; "terra" is the *ex opere operato* fact of self-organized, symbiotic soul/substance, and, "mundus" is the *ex opere operantis* willfulness of soul/substance's self-conscious agency. Because each of us personally is both aspects, (self-organized constructs, intentionally conscious), we are Earth Sacrament, the word/work of God's intentionality in vital Earth substance. The conscious living of this fact is the agency of purposefulness and joyfulness in life.

The birth of a child is a Big Bang experience. It is a new event of creative centering. It is a new *Jesus-coming*. It is a serendipity expression of the miracle of collaborative order/chaos. Parents are thrilled, bewildered and challenged. Parents are in for the education of their lives, in more ways than they can know. Parenting causes one to be exposed to the experience of Godspeak perhaps more than in any other thing. Having one's own child(ren) defines one's lifetime more profoundly than any other experience. Birthing is Lifework, is Godspeak. Parent and child, we are Godspeak and Sacrament to each other.

There is probably only one joy in life greater than that of being parent, and that is being grandparent. Some philosopher grandmother once quipped that being grandparent is so great that there should be a way to go directly to grandparenting without the parenting bit. By now, I am a seasoned enough grandparent to have brag stories to tell; of course, the grandchildren who live closest to their grandparents have the doubtful privilege of being most talked about by their grandparents.

Here are two more recent happenings. Our grandson Gavin is two years old and his brother Foster is one. Their mother is Maria. Maria is college-degreed in speech and hearing impairments; she has a habit of play-acting with her boys. Some weeks back (June 2000) it occurred to her to show Gavin how to penguin-walk. Gavin caught on fast. Tim, the boys' dad, was cultivating corn all day and when he came home Maria wanted Gavin to show his dad what he had learned. So Maria urged, "Gavin, show your papa how a penguin walks." But Gavin was unresponsive so Maria asked him, "Gavin, how does a penguin walk?" Without hesitating Gavin answered, "Mother, he walks with his feet." From Gavin's earliest days Grandma Felicitas ("Grammy") would play with him, and his favorite play with her became pretend cooking. Well, it happened recently that Grammy, Maria, aunt Monica and Rebecca did the garage-sale circuit in Cresco, Iowa, where they discovered a kitchen play set consisting of a clothes washer/dryer, kitchen counter/cabinet/range, etc. Monica made an offer and purchased the set for Gavin. At this same time Foster was transitioning from the crawling stage to the walking, and of course, whatever big brother does he has to try doing. So the kitchen play set caught his fancy, also. Noticing this, Maria suggested, "Gavin, wouldn't it be nice if you let your brother play with you?" Again, without hesitation Gavin said, "But mother, I am not a toy."

If only parents would allow themselves the time to grow up with their children they would be amazed at the wisdom they would acquire—not to mention the joy for their child and themselves. Children need to have their parents do this. On its own, infant/child intelligence cannot alone negotiate the complexities of consciousness. That is what parents and grandparents are for. Certain givens in life, the wisdom of faith/experience, are necessary dimensions of consciousness that go beyond mere intellectual apprehension. They are trust experiences. Such wisdom includes the recognition that from the experience of pain, evil, good can result. This conviction comes at first more from faith-experience than from reason. Parental reinforcement is absolutely necessary for this conviction to become solidified in children. And it is important that it becomes solidified in childhood experience so that a child doesn't grow up being mean-minded and cynical, and reciprocating evil suffered with evil dished out.

Jesus set it straight with his followers when they tried to keep the little kids from coming to him, "Let them come to me. Unless you are like them you do not belong in my company." Jesus was totally fed up with adult pretensions, but especially, with the mindless rules of the temple-keepers. Pretense poisons personal and collective authenticity. When children are raised in a culture of pretense they acquire its shades of inauthenticity. Pretenses are devices of egoism and self-serving. By their culture we are conditioned to be covetous, to seek always the benefit of ourselves without concern for others. Pretense and covetousness promote the culture of scams and con artists. Scam artists are welcomed in high places because culture buys in to scam philosophy and scam ethics. Covetousness becomes the accepted way of life. The atmosphere reeks with distrust and children are made to squirm under it. Religion is covetous. Politics are covetous. Business is covetous. Education is covetous. Nationalism is covetous. We are individually covetous. By our covetousness we teach and exemplify mortal violence toward one another. Covetousness crushes the authentic instincts of children; their violent reaction against this violence should come as no surprise. Children taking up guns and shooting authority figures, including their parents, is their way of reacting to society's trashing the integrity of individual consciousness—every child's birthright.

Institutions tend to fixate consciousness into some averaged absolute and label it "soul." This constriction by absolutism violates the very nature of consciousness, which is essentially elusive, open and fluid. The institutional straight-jacketing of consciousness is for the "objective" purpose of conforming it to serve "orderly" institutional objectives. These devices are ancient practices of "classicism," that is, of the political dividing of societies into two classes, one that rules (enslaves) and the other that serves. The frustration of personal consciousness is a smothering blanket that suppresses intuitive sense and aesthetics. Consciousness is individual and particularized—subjective, but it is at the same time seamless, multicolored and motivating—collectively pooled. To deny consciousness its personal integrity is to bruise and violate it. The creativity of individual consciousness must be revered for its denial does violence to the sacred openness of human nature.

Every newborn is a rebirth of spirit, a resurrection of humankind, a gift of newness entrusted to the living. Perennial life's trust is personalized in the newborn, whose innocence is authenticated in the trustworthiness of the living or is frustrated by its absence. The scandal of distrust is a millstone imperiling Earthlife. Its mortal infection passes from parent to child, from individual culture to societal. The culture of deceit must be challenged, it must be corrected. Challenge and correction happen in the individual heart, in the individual life, which have the power to change other hearts, other lives.

Oh what a grace it is always to be guileless as a child so that one's trust remains transparent for a lifetime. The crime of all time is pretense—the slaughter of innocence.

The answer to the question "Where have we gone wrong?" is that *we do our children wrong*. We give them stones, not bread; we give them stuff, not love. And instead of sustaining syntropy, we bring on entropy. We trash the *middletree*. This answer arises from the deep consciousness of common substantiation. It is as obvious and inobvious as understanding the cosmic harmonics of supposition and opposition, syntropy and entropy. Syntropy is the positive synergy, the subtle transformations of interactive atomic/molecular energies, which enable substantiation; entropy is discord that grounds and frustrates energy's attenuation, radiation and amplification—these are essential forms of communication, consciousness and conscience.

Our own salvation (whole-making) is resourced in deep consciousness, in the deep "poetics" of quantum harmonics, in *the music of the spheres*. Music, like molecular harmonics, is essentially deep centered. Music like molecular poetics, quantum-electric poetics, is radical. There is a physical basis for the fact that music touches feelings that words cannot. Consciousness in substance is the codependent spirituality of quantum-electric bonding. Consciousness is the diversely subtle sensitivity of molecular communication (harmonics). The language common to all substantiation, to all material existence, is the resonance of molecular frequencies—harmonic signaling in quest of reciprocation. In energy attenuation is the experience of all emotion/intelligence. In it we come to an awareness of our true selves. We starve for self-fulfillment except we grow in harmonic experience, in the incorporation of "happy music." Energy attenuation is purposeful to consciousness and substantiation. The producing of music is an *attenuating* exercise whose energy derives from molecular consciousness and amplifies its radiation for further attenuation.

Playing a violin, for example, physically strikes a chord in human consciousness for its resonance is by physical contact picked up in deep body sensation, whose vitality thrills to the experience of energetic attenuation. Perhaps no early learning experience is more vital to lifelong well-being than the personal experience of entering into the deep resonance of music-making—the "song experience." Even more than storytelling, music-making is an excelling religious experience. As the old monastic saying has it, "Quis bene cantat, bis orat" (who sings well prays twice). Story well set to music has twice the impact of story in words only—the power of "quantum poetics." The new universe story needs also to be sung in the attenuating rhythms of its all-encompassing harmony.

SONG IN THE WIND
I dare not importune Mnemosyne
Lest by my clamoring I drown out
Her ever so humble humming.
Rather, I tune my ears
To hear her gratuitous rhythm
That pleases the receptive senses.

ULTIMACY
Nature's supreme I
Must be inevitable,
Unpredictable.

TEA TALK.
Moment by moment, I try,
As faithfully as sprigs sprout leaves,
To pick the select ones from *Poetree* branches.

I enjoy them all, sometimes
Green, sometimes turned and tanned
By Summer's heat, their starch essences stanched

And reduced to their
Essential structures. With boiling water,
Its froth calmed, I alchemize their architectures

And I watch them as
Their timbers explode on contact and yield
Their stellar perfections, their fluid energies,

Their stamina of soul,
Sun-smithen and bracing for every
Situation. The soul of the times can be read

In the temper of Poetree
Leaves. For the times of our lives
The awareness of tealeaves sensitizes ours.

RATIONAL ATTENUATION
(Harmonic Ecstasy)
"You shall draw water joyfully from the springs of salvation"

The Logic of Being is Resonant Emotion.
The Logic of Doing is Resonant Emotion.
The Logic of Having is Resonant Emotion.
The Logic of Loving is Resonant Emotion.
Bliss.. Bliss... Bliss.... Bliss.....

Sylvester L. Steffen

The Subjectivity/Objectivity of Cosmic Religion

In us and around us is a sustaining plasmic sea of cosmic agency, the open oceans of Big Bang energy/substance. This plasmic ocean inhabits the least openness of sub-atomic, atomic, and molecular space, and the vast openness of inter-galactic regions. It is a medium of cosmic continuity, of indeterminate subjectivity/objectivity.

The free-spirit electrons (energetic debris fields) are the agencies of serendipity and subjectivity. Electrons inhabit the skies of nuclei like the atmosphere inhabits Earth; each is to the other subject/object. Included in the electron-complex are photons—the nimble needles of light that collect cosmic strands and connect them in patterns of vital fabric. While electrons come to be tethered in the skies of atomic nuclei, their freedom to innovate, though qualified, is preserved. This is true in the microcosm as it is in the macrocosm. In an unexpected reversal, it seems as a matter of course that electrons enmesh nuclei in their subjectivity work. They do more than let themselves be held in tow by gravity's pull to the center. Their centering agency is specifically a unity-scripture of word/work, of spirituality embodied. The photon is subjectivity's agency of communication/consciousness/conscience. Wave and particle, photons purposefully amass words that work. The place and relationship of electrons are inter-subjective; they "constantly" qualify cosmic relationships (religion) against chaotic destruction.

Every molecular complexity is a subjectivity. The ascent of subjectivity is graduated on subjectivities. Essential developments in antecedent subjectivities qualify new subjectivities. In the progression of transformational life, new expressions of subtleties and potentialities develop out of plateaus of structured uniqueness. The biological term is differentiation. Consciousness also advances on hierarchies of differentiation. Each stage of differentiation is a rung of subsidiarity, a "homeobox," which ladders-in DNA in subsequent expressions.

The expectation of Jesus' promised Second Coming is *photosynthetically* popularized in an open cloud revealing the Sun brilliantly shining. Jesus' First Coming reveals divinity in humanity; his Second Coming reveals divinity in cosmic consciousness—transcendent love consciously transformed out of the ashes of the Big Bang. In every newborn, cosmic Jesus comes again, ever advancing God's love in quantum-electric relationships.

Christogenesis

Transfiguring Humankind. *Christogenesis* is ascendant rebirth that effects the transcendent perfecting of the conscious human in the cosmic continuum. In the ongoing process of Christogenesis humankind is recurrently transfigured. *Transfiguration* is the emotional/intelligent experience of self-perfecting conscience. Transfiguration is an outcome of intentional reflection, a self-conscious experience of harmonic concordance, a *conspiracy* of the divine with the human. While he may not have precisely used the word *transfiguration* to describe his own experience, *harmonic* (ecstasy) *concordance* seems to have been an early and recurring consciousness in the life of Pierre Teilhard de Chardin. He tells in his own words how he came to a reconciliation of the divine with the natural. The following quotations are from the book of Ursula King, "Pierre Teilhard De Chardin," (Orbis Books, copyright 1999, pp. 85-95, Maryknoll, New York 10545-0308 reprinted here with permission).

"...Of the Cosmic Christ we may say both that he is and that he is still growing...(88). Christ is not something added to the world as an extra, he is not an embellishment, a king as we now crown kings, the owner of a great estate...He is the Alpha and Omega, the principle and the end, the foundation stone and the keystone, the Plenitude and the Plentifier... Some Catholics are disconcerted when it is pointed out to them either that the laws of providence may be reduced to determinism and chance or that under our most spiritual powers there lie hidden most complex material structures, or that the Christian religion has roots in a natural religious development of human consciousness, or that the human body presupposes a vast series of previous developments. Such Catholics either deny the facts or are afraid to face them. This is a huge mistake...I am convinced that there is no more substantial nourishment for the religious life than contact with scientific realities, if they are properly understood.

"It is useless, in consequence, and it is unfair to oppose science and Christ, or to separate them as two domains alien to one another. By itself, science cannot discover Christ, but Christ satisfies the yearnings that are born in our hearts in the school of science. (92).

"Let us...give the name of Omega to the upper cosmic goal disclosed by creative union. All that I shall have to say about it may be reduced to three points: A. The revealed Christ is identical with Omega; B. inasmuch as he is Omega...he is seen to be attainable and inevitably present in all things; C. And finally, it was in order that he might become Omega that it was necessary for him, through the travail of his incarnation, to conquer and animate the universe...In order to demonstrate the truth of this fundamental proposition, I need only refer to the long series of Johannine—and still more Pauline—texts in which the supremacy of Christ over the universe is so magnificently expressed. (95).

"In studying the universal Christ we do more than offer the world, whether believing or unbelieving, a more attractive figure. We impose on theology (dogmatic, mystical, moral) a complete recasting...If Christ is to be truly universal, the redemption and hence the fall must extend to the whole universe. Original sin accordingly takes on a cosmic nature that...obliges us radically to restate the historical representation of that sin and the too purely juridical way in which we commonly describe its being passed on. (90).

"Human action can be related to Christ, and can cooperate in the fulfillment of Christ, not only by the intention, the fidelity, and the obedience in which—as an addition—it is clothed, but also by the actual material content of the work done. To realize this very simple fact, in spite of everything, still stands in our present theorizing between Christian and human efforts...for the Christian the whole world becomes divine in its entirety...(90-91).

"We must say of every man that he continues in himself, besides a body and soul a certain physicality that relates in him in his entirety to the universe in which he reaches fulfillment. This is because, strictly speaking, there is in the universe only one single individuality (one single monad), that of the whole conceived in its organized plurality. The unity of measure of the world is the world itself...We have become accustomed to consider persons (monads) as the natural, complete, units into which the world can be broken down. When we speak of "a soul" we believe that we are thinking of an independent reality, coterminous with itself, separable in its identity from other souls and even from the universe. This pluralist concept may well be most inaccurate. (87).

What physical relation...can he (the Christian) find that will satisfy, without doing violence to his faith, his impassioned vision of supreme cosmic reality, present in all things? How can he reconcile in his mind the law of his Church and the law of his heart? Let me point out three successive stages I...went through before I arrived at a satisfactory solution to this interior problem of making one's way to God in all the sincerity and fullness of a soul that is irrevocably "cosmic." 1. The first universal reality, that offered itself to my mind, in the domain of divino-terrestrial forces, was the will of God, conceived as a special energy instilled into beings to animate and order them towards their end...2. I found it necessary to give greater precision to my first approximate explanation (God's will) of the dogma of my own instinct, and so to accept God's creative action as the universal element. 3. ...I found within myself the name that Christianity gives to the universal reality (that) I had worshipped so long: it was 'the cosmic influence (life) of Christ.'" (85-86).

The "intensional/intentional" life of every Christian is "Christogenesis," is the perfecting of human consciousness by ascendant rebirth in the cosmic continuum. The meaning and fact of Christogenesis include the energetic/substantive continuity of cosmic conscience toward ever perfecting self-reflectivity—*Christic* consciousness. More than the physical, historical, person of Jesus, the Christ of First Century History, *Christic consciousness* means also the contemporary rebirth and the enfleshment of perfected/perfecting conscience in the living consciousness of people of all time. Christic consciousness lives in more than one realm, in more than one religious framework. Indeed, cosmic rationality impels it and compels it to become humanly reflective and effective in all realms, in all religious frameworks. The cosmic implication of universal *christic* consciousness states in fact the singular meaning of Catholic-*catholic*. God's will—what Chardin calls *dogma of my own instinct*—is Christogenesis, is the evolution into the mind of Christ and living by it. Christogenesis is being motivated by altruism to serve others, to obey, intentionally and instinctively, God's will, essentially inherent in cosmic relationships (relativity, religion).

Harmonic Ecstasy

Intentional consciousness opens the door for us to an active role in *cosmic consciousness*, Chardin's "noosphere." Practiced intentionality can open the door to personal at-homeness in the cosmos. It was at-homeness in his Father's house that Jesus witnessed to Peter, James and John in the transfiguration event. (Mt.17 1-8; Mk.9 2-8; Lk.9 28-36). By scriptures' mentioning of these Old Testament figures here we might conclude that Moses and Elijah also experienced *harmonic ecstasy*. (Harmonic ecstasy is the emotionally resonating experience of rationality right-with-cosmic-truth.) When our *sacramental* participation in everyday living moves beyond subconscious (*ex opere operato*) passive functioning to self-aware (*ex opere operantis*) active participation, we enter into the intentional realm of putting our lives in harmony with divine (cosmic) intention.

The unified field of vital consciousness (sky, event horizon, *noosphere*) amplifies from simplicity to complexity. Material complexity is the ground-base of spiritual complexity—of self-consciousness. The convergence of cosmic consciousness in vitality occurs by expansion, not by implosion. Cosmic consciousness begins as potential in the Big Bang, and with each subtle bonding (communication-consciousness) a new synthesis results so that the move from *alpha* to *omega* progresses and continues in an unbroken weave of cosmic continuity. The complexity of materiality and spirituality (consciousness) expands with each and every new communication. The expanding consciousness (aura) of the *noosphere* builds on its first simplicity, which endures in the weave of subsidiarity. The weave of spiritual subsidiarity is a trimorphic process, which includes the interactive phases of resurrection, ascendance and transcendence.

Resurrection is a redundant process in which the subsidiary bases of spirituality repeat themselves in new life. Spirituality resides in the psychological potential patterned in the base sequences (C, T, G, A) of common DNA. The DNA bases, while common to all vitality, are virtually unlimited in potential because of their sequencing flexibility. Conscious subtlety (complexity) obtains in material flexibility, which is fundamentally unpredictable so far as we know.

Ascendance is the unfolding (realization) of potential, which is inherently implicate in the nature of flexible linkages. Biodiversity, the diversification of life, expresses in materiality the expanding consciousness of complexity.

Transcendence is a process and quality of spiritual/material sustainability that enables vital wholeness (biodiversity) to secure in base sequencing the essential history of evolutionary consciousness. The *noosphere* is the changing milieu (consciousness field) of coherent materiality/spirituality, which is both subject and object of self-fulfillment.

In his celebration of the "Mass On the World," Chardin (Id, pg. 58) witnesses that he had come to a sense of personal surrender to the higher consciousness of cosmic altruism, his intentional embrace of Divine Intention. The intentional energizing of self-consciousness in the milieu of cosmic consciousness puts one on the path of personal self-fulfillment (salvation), and facilitates communal progress toward Omega (ultimate pleroma). When global consciousness converges *en masse* in cosmic altruism social harmony becomes the work of the masses. It is toward this purpose that the positive energies of the *noosphere* intend, and which each of us should intend in our personal lives. It is a societal imperative to put in place specific educational strategies, which enable parents and educators to heighten in children and in students the understandings of cosmic consciousness and the sacred way of its natural intentionality.

Virtue's Reward

The saying has it that *virtue is its own reward*. This means to say that we become what we intend. If we intend good, and do the good we intend, we are good. We are what we do. The habits of good intention and of doing good become a habit of being good, of being *sacrament* to one another. We become the virtue we do. Being good is an interior inherency, a potential that we receive from the self-perfecting coherency of cosmic expectation (hope), the purpose (will) of *The Good*. Coming to do/be good is a communicationally expressed purpose that motivates the interactivities of subjectivities and initiates in them mutual experiences of Good, the self-aware rationality of faith-trust. (What may be said of virtue may similarly be said of vice.)

The good will of intentional consciousness becomes the habit of intuitional conscience. This psychological cause-and-effect experience makes sense of the saying, "virtue is its own reward." The habit of conscience, sensitized in the habit of the shared experiences of The Good, is the intentionality of communal whole-making, of individual *salvation*, whose effect in the experience of The Good is Love. By living virtuously we become virtuous persons, for in virtue's experience we come to the conscionable ecstasy of *knowing Goodness*— heaven—the experience of Faith-Hope-Love community. The cosmic experience of natural creativity, in process, recapitulates Trinity, the ultimate Ecstasy of Love.

Chardin's Transfiguration (in his own words)

(Source: Ursula King, "Pierre Teilhard de Chardin," copyright 1999, pp. 96-109, Orbis Books, Maryknoll, NY 10545-0308)

"The presence of the incarnate Word penetrates everything as a universal element. It shines at the common heart of things, as a center that is infinitely intimate to them and at the same time (since it coincides with universal fulfillment) infinitely distant...The vital, organizing influence of the universe, of which we are speaking, is essentially grace. We can see, however, from the point of view of creative union, that the wonderful reality of grace must be understood with a much greater intensity and width of meaning than is normally attributed to it...all the processes of the universe are steeped in final purpose, in supernatural life, even to what is most palpable in their reality. (96-97).

"The first act of the incarnation, the first appearance of the cross, is marked by the plunging of the divine unity into the ultimate depths of the multiple. Nothing can enter into the universe that does not emerge from it.

"It is philosophically sound to ask of each element of the world whether its roots do not extend into the furthest limits of the past...not only in ordine intentionis, *but* in ordine naturae, omnia in eo condita sunt, *all things are contained in him, not only, in the order of intention but also in the order of nature. (98-99).*

"...It was the immersion of the universe in the corporeal [image of the sacred Heart of Jesus]*: and an inevitable reaction brought the transfiguration (or transmutation) of the corporeal into an incredible energy of radiation. (101)*

"In a first stage, my mother's Christ [picture] *was in some way 'deindividualized' for me into a form that was 'substantially' hardly representational. But then came a second stage when this humano-divine 'solid' (like my earlier piece of iron and under the same psychic pressure) let up and exploded from within. There was no longer a patch of crimson in the center of Jesus, but a glowing core of fire, whose splendor embraced every contour—first those of the God-Man—and then those of all things that lay within its ambience...*

"At the root of this invasion and envelopment I can distinguish, I believe, the rapidly increasing importance that was being assumed in my spiritual life by the sense of 'the will of God': fidelity to the divine will, by which I mean fidelity to a directed and realized *omnipresence, which can be apprehended both actively and passively in every element of the world and in all its events. Although at first I did not precisely realize the bridge by which this eminently Christian attitude connected my love and my love of things, nevertheless I have always, ever since the first years of my religious life, gladly surrendered myself to this active feeling of communion with God through the universe..."(102).*

"We have seen the mystical milieu gradually develop and assume a form at once divine and human.

"At first, we might have mistaken it for a mere projection of our emotions, their excess flowing out over the world and appearing to animate it.

"Soon, however, its autonomy became apparent as a strange and supremely desirable omnipresence. This universal presence began by drawing into itself all consistence and all energy...

"Sometimes, when I have scrutinized the world very closely, I have thought that I could see it enveloped in an atmosphere—still very tenuous but already individualized—of mutual good will and of truths accepted in common and retained as a permanent heritage. I have seen a shadow floating, as though it were the outline of a universal soul seeking to be born.

"What name can we give to this mysterious entity, who is in some small way our handiwork, with whom, eminently, we can enter into communion, and who is some part of ourselves, yet who masters us, has need of us in order to exist, and at the same time dominates us with the full force of his absolute being?

"*I can feel it: he has a name and face, but he alone can reveal his face and pronounce his name.*

"*Jesus!*

"*The movement that first opened my eyes began* at one point, *in a person: my own person. As my powers of perception were aroused, that point expanded as though it would absorb all things. Very soon, however, it found that the process seemed to be reversed and that it was itself being taken over. Together with all the beings around me I felt that I was caught up in a higher movement that was stirring together all the elements of the universe and grouping them in a new order. When it was given to me to see where the dazzling trail of particular beauties and partial harmonies was leading, I recognized that it was all coming to center* on a single point, *on a person, your person: Jesus!*

"*In his superabundant unity, that person possessed the virtue of each one of the lower mystical circles. His presence impregnated and sustained all things. His power animated all energy. His mastering life ate into every other life, to assimilate it to himself. Thus, Lord, I understand that it was possible to live without ever emerging from you, without ever ceasing to be buried in you, the ocean of life, the life that penetrates and quickens us. Since first, Lord, you said,* "*Hoc est corpus meum,*" *not only the bread of the altar but (to some degree) everything in the universe that nourishes the soul for the life of spirit and grace has become* yours *and has become* divine—*it is divinized, divinizing, and divinizable. Every presence makes me feel that you are near me; every touch is that touch of your hand; every necessity transmits to me a pulsation of your will. And so true is this, that everything around me that is essential and enduring has become for me the dominance, and in some way, the substance of your heart: Jesus!*

"*That is why it is impossible for me, Lord,—impossible for any person who has acquired even the smallest understanding of you—to look on your face without seeing in it the* radiance *of every reality and every goodness. In the mystery of your mystical body—your cosmic body—you sought to feel the echo of every joy and every fear that moves each single one of all the countless cells that make up humankind. And correspondingly, we cannot contemplate you and adhere to you without your Being, for all its supreme simplicity, transmuting itself as we grasp it into the structured multitude of all that you love upon earth: Jesus!*

"*And the result of this astonishing synthesis of all perfection and all growth that you effect in yourself is that the act by which I possess you combines, in its strict simplicity, more attitudes and more insights than I have spoken of here, and more than I could ever express. When I think of you, Lord, I cannot say whether it is in this place that I find you more, or in that place, whether you are to me friend or strength or matter, whether I am contemplating you or whether I am suffering, whether I rue my faults or find union, whether it is you I love or the whole sum of others. Every affection, every desire, every possession, every light, every depth, every harmony, and every ardor glitters with equal brilliance, at one and the same time, in the inexpressible* relationship *that is being set up between me and you: Jesus! (107-109).*

Personal Conversion (Evangelization)

Naturally, the lessons of Jesus' teaching and personal example correspond with the lessons of cosmic religion. The Christian Gospel (evangelization) refreshes the good news of altruistic conversion, of conscious coming together (convergence) in committed service to the commonweal. Evangelization is a consistent rationale of cosmic communication, of correspondence between beginning and ending, between birth and death, and between the Alpha and the Omega. It is in the resurrection-nature of cosmic continuity that as we age individually in wisdom and grace, we physically decrease *so others may increase*.

Convergence involves the *potential* (charged) grounding of opposites, the quantum-electric bonding of positives/negatives. From a psychological (energetic) perspective, *convergence* involves the coming together of differing/opposing understandings. The outcome of the convergence of ideas is an *apocalypse, new light shining* on compatibilities not previously understood. The discovery of a new consciousness can give to both joined opposites a new sense of direction and collaboration not previously understood. By these, human relationships may be better facilitated and frictions reduced. In them, personal "conversion" is enabled.

Toward the betterment of human, social relationships, we all need conversion, conversion away from ego-centrism to altruism, from a consciousness preoccupied with self-interest to one equitably occupied in other-interest. A new consciousness is a conversion from unreflective intension to reflective intention.

This coming together, on common grounds, of opposing understandings to reconciled understandings, is the quantum-electric process of vital communication coming to symbiosis, to relationships of intentional love. Convergence's way, the way of new understandings, may be seen then as a new way of evangelization, a way that does not seek to pit one ideology (culture) against another—which compounds hurtful malignancies—but which symbiotically enables the interpenetration of interests (cultures) on mutually compatible groundings.

With respect to evangelization and cultural antagonisms, common ethics demand that the consumerist deceits of foreign colonials not be exercised to the disadvantage of indigenous peoples; the fact that it has massively occurred, in the centuries of European colonization, now demands redress on the part of those who disproportionately control and use global resources. The removal of an unjust global system (colonial/feudal), which is now in place, is the conscionable obligation of the heirs of those who have put it in place. Nothing less is at stake than the survival of biodiversity and the preservation of sustainable, global resources.

Personal and global commitment to psychological convergence, to the mitigation of fractious polarities, converts intensionality to intentionality. Differences in themselves do not create the problem, indeed, they are a useful and necessary resource for diversification; the failure of good intention to seek out the common grounds of reconciliation, wherein the good contained in differences can be brought to bear for the benefit of all, does cause the problem. When the potential value of differences is negated, it results in a stultifying uniformity that expects and imposes monoculturing. The mentality of sameness, of surfeit, can lead to a passion to obsess and to infect with dullness, disrespect, and frustration toward all objects, including life itself. The culture of quantum-electric openness may contain the remedy for violent pursuits of consumerism and object obsession. This culture of openness may begin with identifying the Christian mandate in quantum-relativity and personal/social civility.

Sylvester L. Steffen

WHITHER CIVILIZATIONS?
Civilization advances on natural civility,
on the interpersonally sustained rationality of
authentic Word-continuity—Intelligence.

The wholesome unity (resonance) of natural intelligence
is a trimorphic rationality—communal vitality's self-advancing
process of communication, consciousness and conscience.

Communication is the express rationale of faith, the
process of making dialogic connections.
Consciousness is the express rationale of hope,
of understanding the implications of dialogic connections.
Conscience is the express rationale of love, the response
of understanding that does what benefits wholesome unity
and avoids unwholesome disunity.

The word/work of whole-making is a rational resonance,
the consilient harmony of faith, hope, and love,
the tri-unity of communal intelligence—*sacra mens*.

IN RESURRECTION the exemplification of faith-based
Communication renews life's (un)certainties in the newborn.
IN ASCENDENCE the exemplification of hope-based
Consciousness animates self-awareness in interpersonal trust.
IN TRANSCENDENCE the exemplification of love-based
Conscience justifies the self-perfecting community.

TRINITARIAN COMMUNITY (family-society) comes to godlikeness
in the exemplification of godlikeness—*intentionally* lived sacrament.

AFTERWORD

Born to be Faithful

I was born into the Catholic Faith of Vatican I. Next to God, the pope was the infallible dispenser of truth, the authoritative interpreter of faith. Every question in matters of religion had an unambiguous answer. The order of nature was as sure and as definitive as the orbits of planets and the rising and setting of the sun—and there was no awareness of the factual incompatibility between planetary movement and the terms *sun rise* and *set*. Living the "Christ Life" was living a life of service to each other. Life was predictable in its final destiny—heaven, hell or purgatory. The matters of spirit were matters of religion and faith, and the matters of nature were matters of science and reason. The two were understood to be worlds separate from one another.

However, in the third decade of my life this secured belief-system would change irreversibly. Discoveries and insights of science exploded on the scene and invaded all disciplines of learning, including theological presumptions. Pope John XXIII opened the windows of Catholicism to the fresh and mind-changing insights of modernity, e.g., quantum relativity. The separate and tidy realms of reason and religion, of science and faith, were no longer walled cities. Their realms began coalescing.

Today I am a Vatican II catholic. I take seriously the literal meaning "catholic," in the sense of being open to the cosmos, to *universal order*, its wholeness and its essential connectedness. Faith and reason, essential in the cosmic process of consciousness, are to me coincident reciprocals of certitude. They reside co-dependently in the common venue of network life, nature's self-aware materiality/spirituality. Matter and energy are a unity even as is the embodied soul of the conscious person. The internal dynamics of their essential co-dependency introduce qualitative and quantitative changes without fragmenting their unity.

The evolving necessities of soul/substance transformation continually reweave rationality, faith as well as reason. Faith is rationally grounded in the experience of trust. Experientially, we know that the providence of nature is trustworthy also to human life, and we also know, or certainly should know by now, that greed-motivated exploitation imposed on nature breaches experiential trust and faith's grounding. Cultured distrust is a millstone throttling civility. The lessons of faith are consciously script in deep nature, and, except the institutional canons of faith are conscionably secured in rational culture, they breach faith and are a public scandal.

Though knowledge's awareness changes, one thing hasn't changed, and that is that living the "Christ Life" is still living personally in the service of each other.

A Testament of Faith

Finally, in my faith-journey, I am a different person today than I was 60, 30, or even 5 years ago. Over time, my faith has become deeper, firmer and simpler, less trivialized. This I know: I am a gift of love, a gift put together by all of life that has gone before me; I am a witness to that love. By "gift" I mean, that in soul/substance, in spirituality/materiality, in mind/body, I am a continuity of the same energy/matter making up all cosmic continuity, all life. God is in, and God is the origin of all love culminating in my mind/body existence.

The intentionality of God's Love is the inherent imprint of consciousness in soul/substance, but especially, in self-aware substance. This gratuity is the greatest grace, the greatest gift. By the conformity of our personal intentionality to God's—discovered in paradigmatic nature, in text and context—we harmonize ourselves in God's Presence, in Love, which alone endures.

In this awareness, one knows that death is but an aspect of birth, and that like birth it shocks consciousness. Death is a necessary step on the way to life's resurrection, ascendance and transcendence; and fear, in the sense of distrusting God, nature, is not a possibility where the understanding of this truth prevails. It is fear, uncertainty, and disconnection that consider death "untimely." Really, in the cosmic perspective, no death is untimely, so we should muster tranquility in its face, and, no matter its circumstances come eventually to celebrate it. All death is purposeful to rebirth, to the transformation of love in soul/substance. We must realize that a vindictive heart is weak in faith. We must rise above the violence of the jungle law of an-eye-for-an-eye and, yes, of a life-for-a-life. Vindictiveness and denial are violent and destructive channelings of energy. Their violence is personally destructive.

I am no longer occupied with faith-trivia, with vain speculations that impose expectations on God. Love's origination of all vitality is the Alpha-Omega of all life—"process" rather than "end." The touchstone word best illuminating the quantum-electric process of subject centering for me is "intussusception," which means also the harmonic reconciliation of life/death, time/eternity. In the essential relativity of the core process of intussusception, subjectivity/objectivity, soul/substance, energy/matter are transformational continuities of beginning and ending (Alpha-Omega). And after individual death what is individual destiny? We know that our body's energy/matter is re-appropriated in Earthlife processing. Beyond that, only God knows. Except, we know also from faith, informed in experience, that a lifetime of individual choosing is with consequences to future personal/communal destinies. The rationality of communal necessity compels personal consciousness to social altruism—caritas—symbioses. In the light of rational consciousness life's expectation seems simple—to seek seriously the resonant consciousness of God's Presence, the expression of Divine Will (Love) in the "scriptural" continuity of nature; and, moment-by-moment, to opt the immediate decision that best resonates Godlikeness. The struggle of informing choice and opting the greater good in personal choosing is each one's personal purgatory. Heaven is the ongoing personal experience of harmonious relationship with God—the resonant rationality that attenuates the power of the Word.

Sylvester L. Steffen

Sylvester L. Steffen

Selected Readings

B. Barnhart, "Second Simplicity," 1999, Paulist Press, 997 Macarthur Boulevard, Mahwah, New Jersey 07430

W. Bausch, "The Yellow Brick Road," 2000, Twenty-Third Publications-Bayard, Box 180, Mystic, CT 06355

T. Berry, "The DREAM of the EARTH," 1988, Sierra Book Club, San Francisco, CA

J. Berthrong, "The Divine Deli," 2000, Orbis Books, Maryknoll, N.Y.

W. Burrows, "New Ministries: the Global Context," 1980, Orbis Books

J. Campbell, "The Masks of God: Creative Mythology," 1968, Penguin Books, Viking Penguin, New York, N.Y.

T. Chardin, "Activation of Energy," 1970, Harcourt, Brace Jovanovich, New York, N. Y.

M. Crosby, "Do You Love Me?," 2000, Orbis Books, Maryknoll, N.Y.

D. Doyle, "The Church Emerging from Vatican II," 2000, Twenty-Third Publications-Bayard, Box 180, Mystic, CT 06355

D. Edwards, "Jesus the Wisdom of God: an Ecological Theology," 1995, Orbis Books, Maryknoll, N.Y.

J. Haught, Editor, "Science and Religion in Search of Cosmic Purpose," 2000, Georgetown University, Washington, D.C.

J. Haught, "God After Darwin: A Theology of Evolution," 2000, Westview Press, 5500 Central Ave., Boulder, CO 80301-2877

J. van Huyssteen, "The Shaping of Rationality," 2000, Wm B. Eerdmans Pub. Co., Grand Rapids, MI 49503

L. Japinga, "Feminism and Christianity," 2000, cokesbury.com

U. King, "Pierre Teilhard De Chardin," 1999, Orbis Books, Maryknoll, NY 10545-0308

C. Mooney, "Teilhard de Chardin and the Mystery of Christ," 1960, Harper & Row Publishers, 49 E 33rd St., New York, NY 10016

C. Quigley, "The Evolution of Civilizations," 1979, Liberty Fund, Inc., Indianapolis, IN

L. Sewall, "Sight and Sensibility," 1999, Jeremy P. Tarcher/Putnam, 375 Hudson Street, New York, NY 10014

P. Sponheim, "The Pulse of Creation: God and the Transformation of the World," Fortress Books, augsburgfortress.org

C. Taylor, "Hegel," 1975, Cambridge University Press, 40 W 20th St., New York, N.Y.10011

P. Tompkins and C. Bird, "The Secret Life of Plants," 1973, Harper & Row Publishers, Inc., 10 East 53rd Street, New York, NY 10022

G. Vanderhaar, "Beyond Violence," 2000, Twenty Third Publication-Bayard, Box 180, Mystic, CT 06355

B Verkamp, "The Senses of Mystery," 2000, The University of Scranton Press, Scranton, PA

J. Wallis, "Faith Works," 2000, Random House, Inc., New York M. Welker, "Creation and Reality," 2000, Fortress Press, augsburgfortress.org

A. Weil, "Spontaneous Healing," 1995, Ballantine Books, A Fawcett Columbine Book, a Division of Random House, New York.

C. Wessels, "The Holy Web: Church and the New Universe Story," 2000, Orbis Books, Maryknoll, N.Y.

Other books by Sylvester L. Steffen

<u>2000</u>: <u>A Summary Prevision toward Global Revitalization</u>
The Prevision indicts the acculturated breach of trust, bad faith, as the root cause of frustrated consciousness, civilizational disharmony, ecological desecration, and the failure of altruistic ascendancy (caritas).

<u>EDEN'S LIFEWORK POETREE</u>: <u>A Reconciliation of Science and Religion</u>
The Reconciliation identifies faith/hope/love as the self-aware rationality (trimorphic resonance) of the psychical/physical processes of communication/ consciousness/conscience, and "sacrament" as the intentional/intensional edification (soul/substance) of cosmic energy/matter. Failed reconciliation, in the historical context, and its consequences in modern times, is identified in essays and poems.

www.secondenlightenment.org

About the Author

Sylvester Steffen is a scientist who is also trained in philosophy and theology. From 1946 to 1957, he studied for the Catholic priesthood with The Society of the Divine Word (S.V.D) missionary Order. In 1960, he completed research studies in the environmental management of stored corn grain and received a master's degree in plant physiology (botany) from Iowa State University. He worked for more than 30 years as a grain scientist, inventor and business entrepreneur. In his retirement years, Steffen began to re-examine the subjects that intrigued him in his youth: cosmology, philosophy, theology and history. He has shared his philosophies in numerous self-published poems, essays and books.

As the father of six and grandfather of seven, Steffen is a firm believer in the school of experience. His favorite piece of advice to the young is: "Don't let school interfere with your education."

www.ingramcontent.com/pod-product-compliance
Lightning Source LLC
Chambersburg PA
CBHW051449280526
45785CB00003B/1489